SEEKERS OF THE SOUL

Seven Psychics and Intuitives Talk about Their Work, and The Lives That Led Them To It

Sherry Ward

iUniverse, Inc.
New York   Bloomington

Seekers of the Soul
Seven Psychics and Intuitives Talk about Their Work, and The Lives That Led Them To It

iUniverse books may be ordered through booksellers or by contacting:

iUniverse
1663 Liberty Drive
Bloomington, IN 47403
www.iuniverse.com
1-800-Authors (1-800-288-4677)

Because of the dynamic nature of the Internet, any Web addresses or links contained in this book may have changed since publication and may no longer be valid. The views expressed in this work are solely those of the author and do not necessarily reflect the views of the publisher, and the publisher hereby disclaims any responsibility for them.

ISBN: 978-0-595-49866-6 (sc)
ISBN: 978-0-595-50112-0 (dj)
ISBN: 978-0-595-61283-3 (ebook)

Cover illustration is a depiction of the burning bush through which God spoke to man.

Printed in the United States of America

iUniverse rev. date: 7/27/2009

The author may be contacted at this address:
Sherry Ward
20235 N. Cave Creek Road
Suite 104-150
Phoenix, AZ   85024
seekersofthesoul.com
sherryward33@gmail.com

CONTENTS

INTRODUCTION

When the *Arkansas Democrat* newspaper in Little Rock hired me years ago, I quickly became their only full-time feature writer. Since my superiors were largely preoccupied with other matters, I more or less had full autonomy: I could write about anything I wanted to. Generally, whatever topic I chose became each week's major Sunday feature. Because I so often wrote about healers, astrologers, handwriting analysts, and the like, one of the editors dubbed me the occult writer (for me, *occult* means hidden). I was surprised that my surreptitious interests were so evident; I thought I had managed to conceal them amidst a smattering of articles about medical conditions, musicians, recreational places, and such.

I have long suspected that anyone with a strong interest in metaphysics, such as myself, is somewhat naturally intuitive. It may be that we simply sense that there is more, that we somehow know things we have no reason to, and that we otherwise carry an awareness of threads of truth underlying such metaphysical arts as astrology, healing, shamanism, divinatory practices, and the like.

When I was diagnosed with cancer four years ago, I already knew from personal experience and exploration that select psychics and intuitives have genuine validity. (Carol Ann Liaros, who teaches intuitive and psychic development, distinguishes between psychic and

1

intuitive: With intuition, you just know; whereas, psychic is using the senses to know.)

Still, when medical science stacked up against my own sense of things and seven medical professionals told me that it was *overwhelmingly* likely that I had cancer, it seemed folly to dismiss their opinions. A series of medical tests had zeroed in on something in my kidney that was described as a solid mass, which apparently smacked of a dire diagnosis.

I eventually calmed down enough to regard my crisis as an opportunity, if not a call, to explore alternative treatments, alternative therapies, and alternative views of the situation at hand, or, rather, in my kidney.

"You have a solid mass in your kidney, and 95 percent of the time solid masses are malignant," the first urologist told me. Mayo Clinic's Web site posited the likelihood of cancer at more like 80 percent.

"Can't you do a biopsy to be sure?" I plaintively asked each of the physicians I conferred with. I didn't want major surgery. I'd had major surgery before, and it was difficult, more so than I'd been led to expect, and it took a year for my energy to return. I took surgery seriously, just as I did the notion of dispensing with a major organ. And removing a major organ without proof of a malignancy didn't seem good medicine or even good sense.

The doctors, however, said a biopsy could be inconclusive, if not misleading. "We might hit a good part," one physician explained.

In my better moments, I thought: *Someone has to be in that 5 percent, why not me?* And in my times of feeling calm and centered, while doing something as mundane as cleaning up the kitchen and not even thinking about the medical matter, I would suddenly be struck with the sense, *I do not have cancer.*

I eventually launched several unconventional searches, but initially I continued to mine the medical field. I went to a Mayo Clinic branch, which was located near my home. I immediately liked the doctor I was directed to see there. As I sat in the motel-room–like examining room, waiting for him to view my most recent film and return, I genuinely expected him to bound back in with good news. After all, I didn't *feel* like I had cancer. I didn't have any sense that something in my body was trying to kill me. I didn't have pain. I didn't even have to pee.

Instead, he returned, seemingly pleased with his certainty about the matter. He said, "My colleague and I looked at your films, and we're pretty sure it's cancer."

He went on to say that he wanted me to have another MRI at their facility, to be reviewed and evaluated by one of their own. Another ray of hope beamed. I kept expecting someone from the medical field to pop up and clarify this mass matter and brush aside my concerns, so that their view coincided with the way that I considered the matter to be: nothing life-threatening and possibly not even kidney-concerning.

Still hoping for a more promising outlook, I went to my general practitioner, a former surgeon and a man I respected. His eyes bugged out at my news—again, apparently something about the words *solid mass* are indicative of big trouble. He referred me to a colleague who was a urologist. That doctor and I struck up a quick and easy rapport, having both graduated from the University of Michigan at about the same time. We got along so well, in fact, that we even tentatively scheduled surgery. I was becoming so daunted with the onslaught of pessimistic opinions that surgery was gaining appeal—just to deal with it, get it over with, be done with it, and be safe.

Reports continued to come in from the radiologists who viewed the various tests I'd been directed to have: an ultrasound, CT scans, two MRIs. Those reports were anything but encouraging. The first doctor kept me in the casket-like-contraption of the MRI so long that I suspected that she was deliberately intending to stir fear in me. Her eventual report read: "a renal cell carcinoma, much less likely ... benign ... encroaching on the lung."

During all of this time, one thing rarely mentioned or asked about was the fact that *I* was the one who asked for a kidney scan in the first place, because I suspected something. Some time earlier, I had had an appointment with a psychic I had never consulted with before, which was unusual for me (if I conferred with one at all, it was with a certain friend; like a lot of people I was leery of psychic readings). The appointment wasn't for health reasons, but because I was seeking guidance during a difficult time in my life. I thought a fresh approach might offer new insights.

That psychic turned out to be a crabby older woman, seemingly new to the remote body scanning activity that a lot of psychics were jumping into. I had a sense that, though somewhat talented, she was not well versed in physiology. I didn't ask about my health during the session, but I allowed her to comment on it as she psychically scanned me from a distance.

"Ooh!" she said toward the end of our session, "You've got something in your bladder. You need to get that taken care of."

I instantly felt that she meant the kidney. Since most of the rest of what she said seemed valid, I considered her pronouncement, though I did not readily act on it or tell anyone. Shortly thereafter, however, I had an appointment for a routine gynecological exam—routine in procedure only, as I hadn't had one in years. Generally I consider myself well attuned to my body and don't often randomly or routinely seek out medical examinations. I made this appointment after meeting the doctor through a second party and liking her. It seemed prudent to have an exam. I have a tendency to develop cysts in my breasts, which later go away. Indeed, while I was at the gynecologist's for the exam, she found something.

"I want you to get an ultrasound on your breast," she said. "I think it's just a cyst. It feels like a cyst, and it moves around like a cyst, but let's get it checked out."

"Okay," I said, and then, as she was writing up the order, I added, "Can you put in a request for them to check my kidneys as well?"

She looked at me oddly of course, and when I was not forthcoming with more information, she wrote up the order without comment.

A short time later I went for the ultrasound. My breasts appeared to look okay, with the concerning cyst already absent. When the technician got to the kidney, however, I noticed that she slowed her movements, and a concerned pallor clouded her face. Round and round she went with the little wand, exploring the area that corresponded to my kidney.

At first the technician tried to make light of her concerns, but after a while she left the room and returned with a physician. They explained that there was something there, something concerning. They discussed it in muted tones. They said they would send the report to my doctor who had ordered the tests. My new gynecologist happened to be on vacation when the test results arrived in her office, so her assistant called and advised me to see a urologist, since kidney was not in the gynecologist's area of expertise. She gave me a list of specialists.

I looked at the names and locations on the list carefully before choosing one. I made an appointment and then arranged for the results of the original ultrasound to be sent to their office. Upon receiving it, they called and asked me to go for a CT scan before I came in. I did as instructed. When it was time for my appointment, the CT film and report had already been sent to them. Theirs was a busy office, and when the receptionist called the brother of a prominent politician before me, I felt encouraged, as if it was an endorsement of the firm I'd chosen.

The doctor's nurse was a brusque German with an utter absence of anything resembling a genteel bedside manner. Of course I wasn't in bed, but still, her icy aloofness was off-putting. She took the films they had given me at the front desk and abruptly exited, leaving a chill in her wake.

When she returned, for the first time I began to feel genuinely afraid. She was suddenly kind, even solicitous. *Uh-oh,* I thought, *I'm in trouble.* A short time later, after lingering, then looking at me with a tenderness I wouldn't have thought she possessed, she exited.

The doctor soon came in and made no bones about it. "You have a solid mass in your left kidney," he said, "and 95 percent of the time solid masses in the kidney are malignant."

I was stunned. I thought a lot of things. *This doesn't sound good. I'll figure this out for myself. I'm a big believer in second and third opinions.* And finally, I thought, *I just want to go home and sort this out.*

It was around this time that I called the woman I conferred with previously, a friend who is an excellent intuitive and an older wise woman besides.

"It's kind of a fatty tumor," she said. "Nothing to be concerned about." And then she seemed ready to change the subject, so dismissive was she. Where others had set off alarm bells, she practically hit the snooze button. I liked it. I was cautious, but I liked it.

Meanwhile I returned to Mayo Clinic to have the other MRI. By the time it took place, I was getting increasingly antsy. I had to drink a radioactive solution, which I could feel illuminate me—and not in a good way. I had a sense before I left the lab that that radiologist's opinion wouldn't differ significantly from any of the others.

Alas, after reading the report, my doctor entered my pleasing examination room, unswayed from his original opinion that the mass was malignant. The radiologist had written: "This needs to be considered a malignancy of the kidney."

I implored the doctor to leave part of the kidney if he operated, and though he said he would try, he advised me that the offending mass was in the center of the organ, thereby making anything less than a nephrectomy—complete removal of the kidney—unlikely.

After that, I took matters into my own hands, eyes, and fingers. I decided to locate healers and practitioners of alternative therapies to see what they could do, while keeping my family and their concerns at bay, and without alienating my physicians.

The doctor at Mayo was persuaded, albeit bemusedly, to give me a window of time in which to explore these alternatives. "Six weeks," he said. "No more." I took him at his word and made good use of the time.

I quietly yet earnestly went about the business of experimenting with different healing possibilities. Some healers I contacted were quite eccentric, including an Englishman severely in need of a bath and a manicure, who sat silently across from me for ninety minutes, doing who-knew-what. I assumed he was performing some kind of energetic healing procedure. He seemed sincere, but I was less than impressed. When he suggested a follow-up appointment, I simply never called him back.

Another woman whom I visited hooked me up to wires that connected me into a computer program that she said would assess me in a variety of ways: emotionally, energetically, physically, and so on. This turned out to be oddly useful, as some emotional issues came up, which we then addressed. I recall that she was surprised by how easily I processed what came up and moved beyond it—even after tears. I had spent much of my life being introspective, so nothing much was unexcavated: I was willing to look at my issues. Since these issues were so near the surface, we correlated what arose with the kidney matter. But physical healing was beyond her realm.

I went to a female physician from China who spoke only a modicum of English. I had been exposed to Tibetan medicine during a trip to Tibet, and I knew that they used some of the same techniques as the Chinese, of checking pulses to determine the health of major organs. She used acupuncture in what sounded like a rather forceful way. From the waiting room, more than once I could hear a woman yell out in pain.

Once I was in to see this doctor, she eyed me dubiously when I told her of my concern. "Kidney?" she reiterated. "Kidney serious," she stated sternly. I gulped internally. She silently checked my pulses in various places, and then the good Dr. Pearl proclaimed, "Kidney fine."

She said it, and I took it as the first medical pronouncement to jive with my own sense of things, giving me a ray of hope to break up the dark clouds shadowing my clarity. She went on to stab me unceremoniously and without tenderness with the acupuncture needles, but I didn't even mind.

I had a positive opinion, two counting my intuitive friend's. I wanted more.

I continued my research on the Internet. I was aware of the work of Dr. Norman Shealy and had loosely followed it for years, as did many of us who suspected that the riches of metaphysics were not being mined.

Dr. Shealy was a Harvard-educated neurosurgeon who began doing research with psychics. He is said to have invented the term *medical intuition* and perhaps the profession as well, along with Caroline Myss, a gifted intuitive, best-selling author, and frequent guest on *Oprah*. Medical intuition is the ability to psychically scan and diagnose or assess a person's physical well-being.

Dr. Shealy began working with psychics, including Myss, at a time when Myss was a rather reluctant intuitive who nonetheless proved uncannily accurate in diagnosing or assessing some of Dr. Shealy's patients. Later, the two constructed a curriculum for training others to be medical intuitives, which is now offered at Holos University. They also co-founded the American Board for Scientific Medical Intuition.

Dr. Shealy's Web site proved to be a rich resource, not just because it offered lists of healers and intuitives, but because of something discovered in his research. According to information I read on his Web site, in his research with psychics and intuitives, Dr. Shealy found that they often disagreed with each other, but when they agreed—when they were in consensus—they were 95 percent accurate.

Ninety-five percent accurate. I was stunned. On the other hand, it actually made sense that if a group of high-quality psychics or intuitives all picked up the same information, that information *would be* highly likely to be accurate.

I set a course for myself. I would locate at least five psychics and intuitives who came recommended on some level and make appointments with them. In order to locate these people, I asked friends, did research, and consulted with respected organizations.

Initially, I made appointments with more than five people, in case some of them fell short of the level of skill I was seeking—if some of what they said simply did not ring true for me.

My plan was to allow the readers to read for me without offering them any information—for them to address whatever came up. If the matter of my health did not arise, then I would ask, "What do you see for my health?" If they gave a general report but did not mention the matter of my kidney, I would lay my cards on the table, so to speak, share what I had been told by more than seven medical professionals (including the radiologists), and simply ask if they felt that the mass was malignant.

I'm not one for making psychics or intuitives jump through hoops. If I can help to clarify a situation, I will. Early on, one of the better ones said at the outset, "Something has stopped you in your tracks." When she then needed me to clarify what was going on, I did. She quietly offered, "You could live safely with this [mass] for the rest of your life."

Five out of the five whose consultations impressed me most said they did not feel that I had cancer.

Of the seven or eight people I consulted with initially, I chose the five who most impressed me. And by that, I mean, for instance, that I dismissed the one who related a rag-tag account of a past life. It didn't matter if she said I had cancer or not (I can't even remember if she did), her reading simply did not ring true for me.

Each of the prized five said that he or she did not feel that the mass in my kidney was malignant. Since I didn't either, I cancelled surgery, stalled my concerned family using Dr. Shealy's statistics about consensus among intuitives, and waited a year before returning for another medical exam. I went back to a laboratory I had been to before. In viewing the ultrasound, the doctor said, "I don't know *what* this is, but it is definitely *not* cancer."

I verily skipped to the car.

The mass had not changed since it was discovered, although there might have been a minute reduction in size. I experienced no adverse effects from it, so I felt safe in allowing it to remain. Two medical intuitives had told me the mass was the result of a childhood injury that should have been treated but wasn't, and that the kidney had created a calcified capsule around the injured area, as if to protect it, and this was what was seen as the mass. They spoke independently of each other and even mentioned the same approximate age when I was injured.

Resting in the relief of the belief that my health was not in jeopardy, I began to think about the seers who had given me the readings. My journalistic instincts kicked in. I wondered, *Who are these people? How did they learn to do this work? What made them think they could? Did they have unusual experiences as children?*

I launched a research project and continued to confer with a variety of psychics and intuitives to see how they worked, what range of insights they were able to offer, and the varying content they provided. I was intrigued. I had a few questionable experiences with persons of dubious intent, but I also found some who seemed able to reach levels beyond life's more mundane matters, into the rarefied parts of me. These were the people who intrigued me most. It was as if they were able to access the loftiest portions of myself, seemingly my soul and its intents and purposes for the life.

I asked the most impressive of these readers for interviews. To my surprise, I found that they were all willing to be profiled. And they were not people who needed business or sought acclaim. I realized that they wanted to tell their stories and share some of what they have learned during their sojourns into the unusual. The information is fascinating and valuable.

I have had remarkable experiences with people who have supernormal abilities. I am interested in demystifying their work, in offering guidance to those of us who are interested in such services, and in suggesting ethics and guidelines for budding psychics and intuitives.

I hope to do justice to the accounts shared by these visionaries.

Sherry Ward

Serafina Andrews
Dancer, Artist, Messenger of Divine Grace

Serafina Andrews is one of those rare individuals in whom the inner child shines through. She speaks softly in a small voice, and her laughter rises up like that of a child's, as if breaking through the glass of adulthood. The child is seen in the sparkle in her eyes, heard in her girlish giggle, and found in her infectious humor.

Serafina was once a ballerina. Now, while in her sixties, she teaches ballet to small children.

"I've been guided to do that," she said, with the satisfaction of knowing.

A small sign on the path into her and her husband's property says, *Slow for Fairies,* and because it looks as if fairies might actually *exist* there, I slowed my steps.

Serafina and her husband, Joel, live near Mendocino, California. Joel Andrews is a well-known and highly regarded harpist, who brings celestial music to thousands of people the world over through concerts and CDs.

The Andrewses live in an original century-old farmhouse, though they added on a room. The property still shows signs of the Portuguese horsemen who homesteaded it. A massive, hundred-year-old cork tree attests to their prior presence.

"They once made cork for wine bottles from these trees," Serafina said, gesturing toward the bark of the tree. "But we won't do that to you," she said, turning back to pat the tree reassuringly.

A small barn out back has been tastefully converted into an art studio for Serafina, who draws and paints.

"She's on her fourth career," her husband asserted proudly.

Dancer. Intuitive. Ballet teacher. Artist.

Serafina's son is an art director for filmmaker George Lucas, and he worked on two of the *Star Wars* movies. His small and sophisticated paintings adorn Serafina's studio. He coached his mother in her art, telling her to simply draw for the first ten years. After working to replicate hands and feet and other body parts for those ten years, Serafina took up oils and now paints.

Her latest subject matter on canvas is the children in her classes. She proudly produced recent photographs of little girls trying on their costumes for a first recital. In their airy attire, they look like tiny representatives of the angelic and nature communities, which Serafina is in touch with, in her work and play.

First Intuitive Readings

More than twenty years ago, Serafina began offering intuitive guidance to others. She had had a sense of receiving guidance from other realms for some time, though it wasn't something she proffered to others. In fact, the first time she gave intuitive or angelic guidance to others was only after she was asked to do so. While teaching a class on communing with angels, students asked if she would answer their questions. She remembers well her early doubts and apprehensions.

"I was giving an *Opening to the Angelic Realm* workshop, along with my husband and a couple of other people … and the group asked if I would … answer some of their questions, and I freaked out! I thought, I can't do this.

"This was the first of the beginning. And I said, 'I'll take … your questions home tonight and I'll bring back answers in the morning.' Well, I was freaking out. I said, 'I can't do this!' and I decided, here I am giving an angel workshop, and I'm the one taking it, you know?" she said and laughed heartily. "And so, I remember sitting down and just shaking all over, thinking I can't do this, I can't do this, and all of a sudden I just calmed down, and I went into meditation, and I heard these beautiful voices bringing through these answers for these dear people that had come to this workshop, and I just started writing them out."

She returned to the workshop the next day, answers in hand to the questions posed.

"We went back to our angel seminar in the redwoods, and it was beautiful, and I was reading these answers back to these people, and they would cry, and it was the most beautiful confirmation. But what was coming out were answers that were universal."

Serafina is clairaudient. She works by writing out information that is given to her, which she hears from those on what she refers to as the *inner planes*, which is her term for this other dimension.

Clairaudience is said to be the ability to hear something outside of the norm. It is often mentioned in league with other paranormal abilities such as clairvoyance, which translates as clear seeing and may be seeing pictures in the mind's eye or literally seeing what to others is not there. Clairsentience is clear sensing or feeling. Claircognizance is clear knowing. Clairsmellience—a term first coined as a bit of a joke—is the ability to pick up smells not normally sensed by others, which can give information about a person, place, or event.

"I really actually call myself a scribe," Serafina said. "When I do sessions for people, I hear the messages and write them out, but within the time of writing it out and laying it out, the people are being healed [on some level]. There's this time, in what I call a state of grace, and in that time is the time where the healing can take place. So there's a reason why I was going to be writing. I always thought, *Why can't I just say the words? Why can't I just be fast?* But that wasn't my work, my gift to give, in bringing out the people. And the reason was to allow for that time."

Messenger of Divine Grace

"I have been doing this work [intuitive readings] for a good twenty-two years, twenty-three years now, and it was a slow guidance into learning and developing this intuition," Serafina said. "I call myself a sensitive, an oracle."

Serafina calls her intuitive sessions *Soul Path Awakenings*. She chose this title because it was what seemed to be needed at the time she formulated the sessions. She said, however, that spirit shifts what's important to bring forth in the world, according to the needs of the time.

In Serafina's series, clients may choose from any of five sessions or request an individual reading in which they may ask three personal questions. The sessions in the series are these:

- How to Recognize Your Spiritual Path
- Healing Emotional and Physical Blocks
- Awaken the Artist Within
- Individualized Healing Meditations
- Soul-Path Blueprints: What Is Your Soul's Highest Destiny?

During the sessions Serafina uses several different questions, which she poses to her guides, in order to obtain the needed information for a given client. She does the healing meditation with her husband, Joel, who provides individualized healing music with his harp for each session. Healing may occur on any of many levels, such as emotional, mental, physical, and spiritual.

Serafina and Joel Andrews were pioneers in the work of offering transformative healings to people through channeling words and music from higher spiritual realms. They also worked with others early to the field of combining metaphysics with science, including Dr. Norman Shealy, a Harvard-educated neurosurgeon, and Marcel Vogel, a scientific researcher.

Serafina was asked how it is that she thinks intuitive readings may help people, and she said if the intuitive is working with divine spirit, it could help the person to get their soul back on track.

"If they're working in spirit, with divine spirit [giving] … that blessing, I think we're messengers of divine grace," she said.

Serafina does the work in bringing through the messages, but she doesn't take credit for the information provided. She said that goes to divine spirit.

"We're humble servants," she said. "And I never ever think of myself … that *I* did this or *I* did that. It's so strange; I don't claim any of it. I never attach myself to any of it. I say, 'Oh that's nice.' I feel it just was a gift [from the divine], through my energy and efforts to help it through. And I'm just a witness, and I'm grateful to be a part of it."

Early Experiences of an Unusual Sort

In some ways, Serafina was always in touch with the other side, with worlds largely unseen. Her childhood was a happy one, and, although she had unusual experiences, she said not much was made of them.

"I was not encouraged in it," she recalled. "No one was aware of it [mostly]. My parents would say that I would know things, but we didn't make any big deal about it. I would know ahead what was around. Or, I remember, more on my own, I would put my hand on a table, and I would just feel all kinds of things that had happened in the past, things going on. I didn't think much of it. I thought, *Oh, that's kind of interesting.*

"I know I was very attuned to nature, and I have transcendental experiences of nature. I remember one time in ballet when I was doing bar work, I just felt like Siddhartha [Buddha]; my face just became rivers and valleys."

Serafina's happy childhood may have helped to keep the child within her strong and clear and close at hand. She lived in an idyllic area and was raised in the world of dance.

"I grew up in dance studios and getting ready for concert tours. I had beautiful teachers, beautiful parents. I grew up in California, out where the buffalo were still roaming. My parents had horses and animals, and it was just so wonderful—peacocks, goats that could climb up trees, all the nature. So I was very blessed."

After a number of years in the world of dance, she began to have experiences that indicated to her that there was more to do, more for her to learn.

"I remember early ages as a concert dancer in ballet, Spanish flamenco. I was dancing but feeling like something was taken from me, and I would feel strange about that, not feeling comfortable after a while. So, something was telling me there was more to learn."

Serafina began to have other unusual experiences as well, which she did not always understand.

"I'm giving you a process of how I got into the work ... I think it's kind of important. I couldn't figure out what the signs were, but I'd go to a student [in dance], and I'd touch their body, and they'd say, 'Ouch, that hurts.' And this was happening for about a month over and over again. I couldn't figure out what was going on, and, again, it was like I didn't quite get it. I didn't understand. But I was very concerned; things were happening."

She believes now that she was being led to intuitively touch places on the dancers' bodies where healing was needed.

"The 'ouch' was a place on their body where people had pain and needed healing," Serafina explained. "It was a wake-up call for me in the early years, to find out what this was about, and it led me toward more understanding of healing on the emotional body years later."

Although Serafina had unusual experiences prior to meeting her husband, she credits him with expanding her possibilities and helping her to be open to still more, through his harp, which helped attune her to higher levels.

Theirs is a love story seen in their eyes still. When they met, Serafina was just beginning to feel called to higher work, and she remembers well her development and the part Joel was to play in it.

Finding Her Spiritual Partner

Joel and Serafina's initial introduction seems to suggest celestial orchestration. She enjoys sharing the following story, she said, mostly for the fun of it. She laughed joyfully in recalling how they first were brought together during her spiritual search more than twenty years ago:

"Finally, the most motivating part was realizing I really wanted a spiritual partner, and that my life was shifting and that I had higher work to do, and so that's when the journey really started, when I realized that, in the work, it would be wonderful to be with a spiritual partner. So I started praying, and I prayed and I prayed and all of a sudden I had this vision … and they said, 'You will recognize him by his smile.'

"All right, I'm having a heyday, I'm having a wonderful time, because everyone I meet, I'm thinking, this could be the guy, this could be the man in my life …

"This is when I lived in the Santa Cruz Mountains. I had a little house up there, and I played the harp … a folk harp … and one night I was out on my deck, it was a very beautiful summer night, and I heard another harp from across the mountain! I thought, *Oh, there's another harp in the valley! I can't wait.*

"The next morning the harpist shows up. 'Were you the lady playing the harp last night?' I said yes. Well, we start talking, and I was so excited about what he was saying about healing with music and that was what my dream was. I really was touching into being a healer and wanting to do more with healing and the healing arts. And here was somebody coming to my doorstep! To guide me.

"He said, 'Well, I know one healer with the harp and it's Joel Andrews.' And I said, 'Oh that's wonderful, a harpist I could go and meet and study with.' And two days later I met another person and they're saying, 'Oh you're interested in healing and harp? You are? Well you must meet Joel Andrews.' This happened three times within the week. And it was obviously a big sign.

"Somehow or another, I ended up meeting Joel Andrews and offering to have him come up and, well, I had a reading by him on the harp, and it changed my life. He gave me keys to unlock my whole spiritual steps forward. It was amazing and very transforming.

"After that I was so excited and I said, 'You must come up to Santa Cruz, and we'll put a concert on for you.'

"I had never talked to ministers before, and I'd been a flamenco dancer out in another world, and all of a sudden I'm putting on a concert in a church, and so from that moment it was changing my vibration. I was beginning to be in tune with healing, and I wanted to serve and that was the main thing that made the difference. My heart wanted to serve and not just entertain anymore. Entertaining took me to a place, and it was wonderful, but it wasn't really giving the way I wanted to give, so at that point I really dedicated myself to service. I think that was the key [to] opening to the transformation, and the intuitive opening coming."

Afterward Joel did come to Santa Cruz, and they fell in love.

"And he had the most wonderful smile," she said, smiling herself in remembrance. "So, he was one of my most wonderful teachers for the spiritual healing work."

They have been together for twenty-six years.

"The journey just keeps beginning over and over again with amazing things happening," she said.

"After we met, I decided it was time to give up my dance career, and I wanted to tour with him, so we started traveling all over the world, and we were traveling six to eight months a year, on concert tours, healing tours, workshops, you know, everything you can imagine."

Their travels have taken them to Europe and Asia, where they have both served—he as a celebrated harpist, and she as his wife and an inspired poet and intuitive.

The Readings as Seeds, Charging Fees, and Predicting the Future

Serafina offers various intuitive sessions. Each is aimed at generating positive possibilities for the clients.

"Those are just guidelines, they go way beyond that. People have all different kinds of questions, so those [session themes] are just to help people get an idea and sometimes they [guides] use those, which are just incredible, to tap into their creativity, their soul path purposes. They're all very, very valuable readings or sessions, because they're like seeds.

"It's almost like I'm working on the subconscious, and it's like the seeds are being planted. They [clients] hear, you know, a suggestion of their highest potential. They may not be ready for it. Not even for this lifetime perhaps, but they hear it. It's planted, like a beautiful garden. You have to put the seed in before you get the plant. And concepts and pattern shifting and energy shifts are not something that happens overnight. People think they can come to me and totally have an instant [and she snaps her fingers] healing, but we've set these patterns, and we have to be totally vigilant in wanting to change the habits of the

...erns. No one can do that for you. It has to be from your own will, and your own desire. And that's the path toward peace for you."

She remembers the first time she ever dared charge for a reading.

"Oh, that was so hard," Serafina recalled. "But, as my husband said to me, 'You know we don't charge for the reading, we charge for our time.' We have to make our way out in the world too. We're given this gift ... so it's mostly the time we spend with the person, not the information that comes through. Because I think that's a gift everyone deserves."

She and her husband have been called to perform the world over and needed the finances to get there. When Serafina and Joel give readings together, he works through his music, playing intuitively by attuning to the divine, and she functions as a scribe, giving inspired writings.

She has made her peace with the need to request fees.

"We couldn't get to Europe," she said cheerfully, "without having a way to get there. We couldn't go to any event without having some way to afford it. No one's paying for it unless we ask for it. So I don't think one should be shy about it. I think they should just be respectful, in that it's [our] time, and do they value their time."

However, she tries to find a way to give the gift of the work to those who are financially challenged and unable to pay.

"I always say to people, if it's not affordable, then let's do another way, a trade or something. I never hold back. Because I feel, again, I want to see people happy."

Though Serafina does believe intuitive guidance can help others, she is leery of predicting the future.

"I never tell the future," she said. "I always think that if any intuitive starts telling futures, watch out ... I've been taught that we can *suggest* potential for this soul, but to dictate its direction would be playing with karmic patterns. And so, with the work I was bringing through, I realized more and more, it was about spiritual wisdom and showing a soul their highest potential.

"I feel that we have free will, and if you interfere with that free will by giving a statement of, 'You must do this or you have to go there or you should live there,' you're interfering with free will and that's a big responsibility. I wouldn't want that one. But you can suggest.

"And may the guidance be in divine spirit's blessing, right?" she added.

Getting in Touch with the Divine

Learning to tune in to be in touch with our own divinity, Serafina said, is a very individual process.

"Everyone's different," she said. "And many times, it takes first clearing a lot of karmic patterns and … it could be on all levels. It just depends on the individual. There's no specific answer for this question. It's an individual journey … that brings the soul to its highest potential for this earth life and for the journey into eternal. It's a pure vibration of attunement with your truth, your own truth, no one else's truth, because everyone's truth is right."

Still, she gave a description of her own process, for tuning in to do a session for a client.

"I would have to find myself a place that's a sanctuary within myself, and I would establish a vibration. Even if I'm rushing in a room when I'm touring, I have to establish a vibrational harmony within myself and within the room or the place that I'm going to be working in," Serafina said. "And I say two affirmations: one to release anything that's not for my highest good or the highest good of the person I'm going to be working with, and another for protection.

"And so the affirmations are sort of a way for me, and a symbol of opening up, to what I call a state of grace. And in that state of grace, I step aside from myself. I step aside from time and world situations and everything. I'm in this grace, and this then allows permission for a higher divine consciousness to work with me and through me."

Serafina gave an example of an affirmation or prayer she might use at the start of a session with a client, so that she might be directed to say the right thing and be in tune with the right vibration, and be protected.

> *Father/Mother God, we reach out in love and light and we ask that [we] both be cleared and cleansed in the universal white Christ light, in the green healing light, and in the ultraviolet transmuting flame. Within God's will and for*

*our highest good we ask that any negativity and evil be
totally removed now from this room and from anything
concerning this issue. I call forth the holy brothers and
sisters of the light to seize it, bind it, and render it inactive
so that it cannot be reestablished within ourselves or
anyone, and we give great thanks for this time together.*

During her spiritual search, Serafina said that she didn't read a great
deal, which was almost intentional, because she didn't want to dilute
the experience or influence the information coming through her.

"I remember, I didn't read a lot about channeling with angels and
all of this, and it was almost on purpose because I think, at this point,
if I had studied a lot of stuff, it would have just interfered with the pure
wisdom that was being given," Serafina said. "But I did one day pull
out a book … I never looked at the book before, but it was on the shelf;
my husband has wonderful books that he's studied … and I started to
read his book on angels, experiences [the author] had with angels, and
I flipped out because it was the same kind of words and phrasing and
the way he talked about it that I was experiencing, and I had never
ever read his book. So there again, it was saying there's this beautiful
continuity coming through."

When Serafina does her work as a scribe, she feels she is in touch
with the divine, regardless of the word one wishes to use for it.

"I see it as being the most beautiful hope and upliftment that we
can reach for, and I see them as messengers and guides and protectors,
guiding us to the right place at the right time, for the right reason. And
you know, they could be angels—I think the word may shift but it's
always there. Whenever divine spirit, holy spirit, whenever you attune
to that kind of vibration, that's all part of the angelic realm … But how
can you put words to something so divine?" she mused dreamily.

"It's really teaching people how to find their divinity," she said.

Ultimately, she thinks our purpose is to be in touch with the
divine.

"As far as what is our purpose?" she posed. "It's ultimately connecting
with divine spirit. Isn't that what we're up against when we think about
our world? We're being pushed to the edge …Wake up and maybe
it's all for a great purpose, to find and connect with what I call divine

spirit, whatever word, whatever modality of spiritual belief you have, there's a word for it. I like to see that we rise up out of it to one unity and work from there, to bring forth our highest potential on the earth plane."

In her readings she hopes to present people with the seeds of their highest potential, whether those seeds sprout in this life or another, which begs the question about reincarnation. Serafina embraces it, but thinks others should only if it works for them.

"I think it's a question of, if it works for somebody, great, but I'm not attached to saying yes or no about that; I'm still evolving. But I believe in it [reincarnation] … I never hold anything too definite because life is going so fast. I'm discovering."

Although Serafina offers her work as a scribe, intuitively communicating with higher spiritual realms for people seeking guidance, she actually believes no one truly has our answers but us.

"It's interesting, whenever I ask spirit, 'So, what's happening? … ' And they're saying 'Be calm, be peaceful, because in your prayers and in your meditations you're protected, and if ever you want an answer, all you have to do is go within, because no one else has the real answer for you.' And all healers and all of the intuitives that are helping, bless them all, because they're all doing their part, and all they're trying to do, on a higher level, is help everyone find this place within themselves so they can know they're divine."

Finding Her Way to Working with Higher Realms

Early in her spiritual development, Serafina had experiences and visions, which showed her that there are other planes or dimensions where illuminated beings exist. She had visions of "inner temples."

"I think the book that was so amazing," she told me, "when I was beginning to open up I was in a bookstore, and I was asking for guidance—always a good thing to do—and I just walked to the back of the store. It was Gateway Bookstore, and there was this golden light around this book, and my hand just reached out, took it down. I didn't even look at the title. I said, 'I'd like to get this book.' I went home; it was *The Brotherhood of Mount Shasta*. So, I mean, I was new to all of this."

Some people think that the Brotherhood of Mount Shasta is the same as the Ascended Masters. The Ascended Masters are said to be the guardians of humanity working from higher levels or what some refer to as the inner planes. They include high spiritual beings known from humanity's history, such as Jesus, Buddha, and the like. Mount Shasta in California is considered by many to be a spiritual enclave. The masters can be contacted there, some people say, physically or in meditation or through transcendental experiences. Mount Shasta figured prominently in Serafina's early spiritual life, though not always in ways she clearly understood. Still, she found her way.

"Before I was even aware of any [inner] temples, I was seeing and dreaming—seeing them in visions so I knew something was happening. And the messages that came through were always, like, with St. Germaine [an Ascended Master].

"My openings into Mountain Shasta in the early days and going into the mountain in the inner planes was so extraordinary," Serafina recalled reverently. "At that time, before I met my husband, St. Germaine was deeply very active in my life, I mean, I was very tied with particular masters. I don't know how many sensitives now work with the Ascended Masters, but they're very much working with us. So I think I was being very guided to get more *aware* of what this was all about. I had no teachers at the time. I was on my own, it was really hard, and I didn't know who to go to because I didn't know the questions."

Serafina spoke of what she considers the importance of Mount Shasta to be, or to have been at one time perhaps.

"It's one beautiful symbolism of divine spirit connecting with the earth; you could put it like that. I'm sure there are a million ways to express it and a million people who could do it better than I. To me it's like … a vortex of symbolism for us, but it's also a very real inner planes connection with spirit. And it may have shifted, I don't know. It just depends. There are many other places like this that are very spiritual and [have] very powerful vortexes that hold records that create spiritual reverence. It just depends on who the person is searching for. Because, in the inner planes, we travel all over."

For Serafina, the persona referred to as St. Germaine was to be of vital importance in her spiritual life. St. Germaine is said to be an

Ascended Master who is in charge of a particular department of life governing man: that of using ritual and ceremony for spiritual work and development. As it turned out, Serafina's husband-to-be, Joel, was in touch with those levels as well, and with St. Germaine in particular, and in time he would help Serafina to open to a greater extent.

Joel channels music said to come from St. Germaine, including healing and protective music, which brings in what is called the violet transmuting flame, which is described as an ethereal force that can positively alter the quality of energy. Energy is generally neutral until we "qualify" it by our thoughts, words, actions, and the like. St. Germaine's specialty is providing the violet transmuting flame to transmute or change negative energy to the positive and, thereby, provide protection and positive change for the planet and its inhabitants.

Ironically, or perhaps not, Joel and Serafina were *both* familiar with St. Germaine before they met, though in different ways.

"Well, my husband would channel St. Germaine ... and I realized through the concerts I would have so many inner planes experiences with his music and so many beautiful experiences with the angelic realm. He was such a conduit—he is—of bringing through this energy of the angelic realm that it was natural. Especially in the early days when we were together, he would channel St. Germaine, and that's when I became attuned more and more with those beautiful energies. And I just know my experiences going into the inner planes and the temples of Mount Shasta, the experience of just being bathed in these incredible rays of love, totally total love, cleansings at the soul level, to even come into that vibration [was a privilege]."

Serafina feels now that the names of those guides she works with are not as important as they once seemed to be. What *is* important is their connection to the divine and the level of vibration they operate from.

"You asked a question, who are my guides, and I think that's important because, for a long time I realized people were very attached to, 'Well, who was it? Who is it?' And more and more, I was being told that it's not so important, the names. I mean, it would be a host of angels, or the Christ, or the Ascended Masters. It wasn't so much identifying what that particular, you know, divine spirit was, it was the *ultimate* divine spirit that was coming through and being the guidance. Isn't that beautiful?"

As for her guides, she does have the sense that they change from time to time, which pleases her, as long as they remain within the ranks of divinity. And she takes steps to insure that this is so, through prayers, affirmations, and the like.

"They shift every once in a while," she confirmed, "and it's been glorious."

Being Tested and Dealing with Dark Forces

"Before I met my husband … I met some people who I thought were very, very spiritual, and they just hooked on to me like crazy, and they invited me up to their home to play the harp, and everything looked just totally incredible. But I was being tested. I was swept away by—I'm not going to mention institutes, but they were very impressive. I'll only tell this one story because this was a hard lesson, but it was something I got through," she told me.

"There were many hard lessons of brushing with dark forces because they come in and they love to take over. Well, I realized something was strange about this situation, and I started getting symbols, and a few nights later an energy came into my home at night and just turned it upside down. I mean it was like a hurricane hit my house on the inner planes … I thought I was going to blow out like Dorothy in the [Wizard of Oz] … All of a sudden I prayed to spirit, I said, 'Please help me,' and all of a sudden I heard my harp playing—it was in another room … and I ran out there, and there was nobody there. But everything got very calm all of a sudden.

"I'm just saying … I was making choices on who to believe and how to understand the guidance of which way to go. But I had come in contact with some black, black—I think black—what would you call dark forces? I didn't know anything about this stuff, although in past lives I may have had this [knowledge] before. But I realized there and then that I've learned to attune with the spirit of the divine and the angels … And so from then, I was more attentive to the symbols, and I would start picking them up; it was my protection."

Serafina said dark forces will reveal themselves, though in sometimes subtle ways.

"Like, you could look at a painting of a spirit, a master, or something, and then look down at their shoes, and one is red and one is black or something. That's real obvious, but the dark forces will always reveal *something*. I only say this because this was my experience to see symbolism even though you *think* they're working in the light, they might have a dark cross on the inner planes, a dark cross on their hand. I just say this for some souls that might pick this up, and it might be helpful."

Serafina said these experiences can be during meditation, but they don't necessarily have to be.

"You could be walking in a room and be overwhelmed by the beauty and glory of it all, and yet, something is not right," she cautioned.

"I remember—this is important for beginning intuitives—we would have meditation groups at our home and healing circles, actually a healing center at that time in our home. And once in a while I would feel really strange, and then I would have an argument with my husband after these sessions [ended] and … we finally figured out that I was so open that I was attracting entities [released in the healing sessions perhaps], and it was affecting our relationship and affecting what we were doing.

"So I really realized how important it was to say affirmations and protect yourself whenever you're bringing through information, spiritual information, that's going to help another soul or yourself, because, as I've learned through many sources, many intuitives, dark forces do their best work right up against the light."

There is in fact an ancient precept in esoteric circles that the dark always attacks the light.

"I just could go on and on with the evolution of *learning* these things," Serafina said. "Before I met Joel, the testing, and the people that were coming into my life. As soon as you want to be in service—I mean, it's a big responsibility. I protect the portals and all the energies that could interfere with what I call the violet flame."

She believes that dark forces can be active in tempting and testing people on the spiritual path. For others, perhaps there was something in a past life that attracts these forces to their current one.

"First of all, it could deal with past lives that you've had, if you believe in that, and it could be your karmic pattern to be attracted to learning a certain way, and the dark forces can play a big part in tempting you, especially if you have psychic abilities and that," Serafina said. "They could go off and persuade things to happen that might be detrimental to a soul. So that's why the affirmations are extremely important.

"No matter how great a psychic/intuitive you are, there's never a time that you can be off guard. Because we're always being tested and, of course, if you're bathing in the light of divine spirit, you *are* being protected. I'm not trying to scare someone. I'm just trying to say it's extremely important [to be discerning and protected]."

She believes through her disconcerting experiences that she was being taught to be discerning, and she shares this account only in the hope that it might be of help to others faced with similar challenges.

"And so, enough of that," she said, signifying that that was the end of this subject. "I'm sorry, I just *had* to bring that up, only because, it's not easy all the time to be a channel, and you constantly have to—in the beginning stages, the affirmations, I only want to say again, are part of the protection."

Serafina has since learned the importance of using discernment and of asking for and using protective techniques.

"So now it's been wonderful," she said happily.

Being Prepared to Be a Scribe for the Divine

Before she began her work as an intuitive scribe for others, Serafina worked on herself. She received healings, many that her husband was instrumental in orchestrating. Joel Andrews was, then as now, well known for producing music channeled from higher spiritual realms. He even gave past life readings through music, producing what might be described as a symphony of the soul. While working with Joel in the earlier years, Serafina was attuning and growing.

After their marriage, she made a conscious choice to step behind the scenes and to travel with her husband as he performed throughout the world. Before they embarked, however, she declared her desire to be of service, and she thinks that this action mattered.

"Just before we started to [travel] … I went to an incredible workshop … it was a whole workshop on prosperity. At the end of the workshop we were supposed to stand up and proclaim what we wanted to do with our lives, and I stood up out of nowhere and—having fifteen women looking at you and you have to say something, I don't know where the words came from—I said, I want to be an emissary for peace. And the next day, we get calls from Japan saying, will you come over to Japan, and back then it was really rare … that the spiritual movement had been over to Japan … in that new way, the new way in spiritual healing. So here we go and all of a sudden, this emissary for peace [idea] just started to take off … It was in the proclamation.

"And so that was a motivating force for the beginning of my work, my psychic work, and healing work."

Serafina believes the declaration set the stage for her intention.

The Wisdom for Us to Connect with, Through Intention

Serafina believes that divine wisdom is there for us to connect with, if we do it with intention followed by action.

"The wisdom is there, for us to connect with. It's all about the wisdom," she declared. "It's not just learning it intellectually, it's integrating it with action and belief and purpose. And I think the most important thing is, what is your intention. Because through the intention you create the cause. Through that motivation you create the cause and then the action, and if it isn't honored grounding that's going to support you, for me, in a spiritual way, then it's going to be out of balance, and your life will not be in harmony. If your intention wasn't right in the beginning, it will create a lot of mischief. And maybe it's appropriate for lessons. So there's no judgment in it. Maybe you take the roundabout way, the long way journey home, or maybe you take the happy journey home, you know? It just depends on how you set it up. And before you come into this life pattern, I do believe that you have decided ahead what your pattern in the journey is."

In addition to Japan, Joel and Serafina were asked to perform in Europe, where they often went. Serafina did a great deal of work behind the scenes, selling Joel's CDs and spending time with others with spiritual insights and abilities. After her previous time in the limelight, she found it pleasing to be in the background, being useful and supportive.

"Because," she recalled, "I was really observing. I didn't realize it at that time, and it was incredible training for me, to hear and meet the people, to see where they're at, and, after a while, I started saying, 'I think you need this music' or 'Maybe you should go here' or 'Maybe you should do this.' They were asking for suggestions, and it just kept kind of being pulled out of me more and more ...

"The more we traveled around the world, the more *I* did readings for people, and it was incredible," Serafina recalled. "Mostly, in the last fifteen years, we've been in Europe, a lot in Europe, and people were very open to that, more accepting of being given a channeled reading or an intuitive reading and not so doubtful as we were in this country. But that could vary for each sensitive, too; but in Europe we would do a concert, and then we would do sessions for people, and my training came from doing sessions for people on all different levels, from doing sessions on people for cleansing entities, doing past life karmic pattern sessions [and other types of sessions]."

Serafina is among those who believe that entities can attach to living persons, to the detriment of all parties.

As a self-proclaimed emissary for peace she was also called on to do work that she might not have consciously chosen, for it involved some unpleasantness.

"When we were in Europe, I remember sitting in cathedrals and feeling souls come up out of the floor, and I realized these were locked souls that hadn't been realized. That was really something. So what it turned out to become was rescue work [for lost souls], but I wasn't aware of that for a long time, until I started seeing these patterns.

"They were souls that had crossed over but were locked in an inner planes situation where they couldn't be released; they weren't ready to go on yet, they were still here, and for a while I did this with my husband too; he was helping me."

Serafina believes that there are earthbound souls or entities who, for one reason or another, have not gone on to the realms where they are most suited to be, and it has been her work at times to help to release these souls that they might move to a more appropriate realm.

"I remember in Sonoma we were in a mission, and I experienced all these souls, lost and in a kind of very painful place, and I remember writing poetry about it first, not knowing what I was doing, but realizing after a while, I was working with these souls, helping them be released. The same thing happened in a number of places [describing a place where there were once whalers like in the book *Moby Dick*] ... There was a little church there where the sailors would go to pray before they went out to sea. That was so incredible, feeling all those souls tormented.

"I didn't ask for that! But, you know, that's healing work. Sometimes we're given assignments where we're not saying, 'Well, this is fun.' But it's beautiful, because it's healing work," she asserted.

"And another thing I've learned from my husband especially, telling me this, is that you can't heal everyone. And the thing that I always learned is, ask divine spirit to send you the people that you can truly help."

Healing and Learning, Often in Unexpected Ways

Serafina is among those who believe that discarnate and negative entities can and do attach themselves to others, to their detriment. She met at least two women during her travels in Europe who taught her healing techniques and helped to open her to the work of healing others of such unfortunate situations, which she later used at home.

"I had one case that was a gentleman; I've never had that happen before, but before he was coming in the door [of the house], I felt I had to do a quick exorcism, and it was powerful; it was so powerful. I was shaking in the sense of wow, this is up-stepping a lot of energy here from what I'm used to, and then he came in. And I worked with him for a number of sessions, and he's so beautiful ... But yes many people don't know they're filled with the empties or things that have attached to them, and they can't understand why everything's going wrong. So I've done a lot of cleansing and clearing.

"It just depends on the person. Sometimes I can just actually, just rake it out of them, or use energy of the hands pulling out and cleansing and clearing out a certain area, or I'm guided to just put my hand out and let the radiation of spirit come through to a heart level, or wherever it is on a physical level. Or many times it's a past life.

"It's so beautiful, depending on the person and what they can comprehend, because it's a big deal you know?"

Judge Not, for Ye Know Not, and Only Help Those You Can

No matter what, it is vital not to judge another, Serafina said, for she does not know what their learning is or what their journey has been.

"It's always important, for my learning of this, never to judge a person. No matter how bad it looks on the outside, you have no idea where they've come from," she said.

In giving a reading, Serafina said her guides might tell the client a story that evokes some understanding from them and thereby releases blocks in their energy patterns.

The guides, she said, may tell a client "a story that may or may not be their past life, but it's a story that they can understand, that relates to their situation, and they can understand why the block is there. And they'll often reveal a past life for them, so they can really let go of it. And this helps to release the blocks, just things that have happened because of a misunderstanding, silly little misunderstanding, a misconception, that'll throw a whole life off. But then, it's so beautiful because then they have this journey back to divine spirit, and they have to struggle until they get the message again. And they may live three or four lifetimes, struggling, going through the worst conditions in life, but ultimately they have the choice, you see?"

She said another important thing that she has learned is not to take on another person's "stuff" and to respect their journey as one that they have chosen.

"Another very important point in my learning is never to take on the karmic patterns of another soul, at least from my perspective. Now, others may be able to do that, you know, great gurus and masters," she said and laughed, as if to suggest that *they* are up to the job of it. "Jesus, whoever you want to call a great master. But I do think that for giving that information to people, like a mother who has a child and they feel responsible for their child … or that husband or that mother, whoever it is you're concerned about, let them know that that [person] has come into the world, [and] it truly is a divine journey for them. And that it's not our responsibility to take on other people's journeys. That's a very important lesson I've learned."

She feels people should understand and respect the fact that each soul chooses his or her path.

The Importance of Prayer

Serafina was always somewhat in touch with the other side, with worlds largely unseen. For people like Serafina, doing intuitive work may come fairly easily to them, for there has long been a knowing that *more* exists and a belief in forces beyond, both those of the divine and those that are not.

Serafina was asked how important prayer is in her life.

"I think to find a place to center yourself is a beautiful gift that you can develop for your own well-being ... if you call it prayer or meditation," she said. "Prayers are so powerful.

"I believe in prayer circles and working with other people, energizing. For years we had prayer circles. They were healing circles. Forming circles like that are so powerful right now. Just building energies and creating a beautiful temple space in your home and gathering other people together to do prayer work is a beautiful service. I can't think of a higher thing to do than good thoughts going out of a room.

"I remember [Paramahansa] Yogananda [author of *Autobiography of a Yogi*] in his works saying that every negative thought is exploding above us like a black cloud. Imagine if you're open to just anything, picking up all those thought-forms, which we are so susceptible to. So prayer and meditation is a way of building force fields, you know, to protect you from a negative influence."

Prayer is vital in her work, whether it be prayer or an affirmation, she doesn't ever do a reading without beginning with beseeching the higher to attend her and her work.

In Giving Readings for Herself and Others

When she seeks guidance for herself, Serafina uses the same basic technique as when she seeks insights for a client. In all such instances she is in touch guidance from the other side or what she calls the inner planes.

"I use the same process," she said. "I have a place that is sacred that I sit in, a place … a room or [other] … and I open up to spirit by first saying prayers and affirmations … and I ask to be protected. And then I … ask usually three questions. Okay, going for myself or for anyone, I find for this work that they'll answer them in their own way, but it's almost like permission to open the Akashic Records [to ask those questions]."

The Akashic Records are described as a living library of all we have done, thought, said, and otherwise lived, in this life and beyond. Many times in readings, information from former lives comes through for the client, Serafina said, because once her prayers are said and she is in attunement with the divine, this gives her permission to access the Akashic Records. These records are in the etheric, on other planes of existence, and can be accessed by those permitted to do so.

"I understand [the Akashic Records] as … different vortexes where the records are kept. They can go through files and scan bodies and understand what's going on for a whole life stream, not just this life, and see a soul pattern. So Akashic Records are the storehouses of this amazing wisdom of information. So, with that, with those questions [that she asks], it then gives me the permission to open what I call the Akashic Records and bring through information. That's basically how it's done.

"And if I'm doing long distance sessions for people, I'll put it on tape for them. It's so beautiful. And then after … a session, you can counsel, and people can ask you direct questions and then the information comes directly through me. But it's that basic meditation from writing it, that the healing, I believe, is transmitted."

Healing is an integral part of Serafina's work, and she feels healing can occur on many levels. In her readings, sometimes information comes out in a way that will evoke a positive change for a person, even though that may not seem to be the information the person was seeking. She sees this as being orchestrated by higher guidance.

"I don't think the sources would give me anything unless it was important to know about," she said. "Or they would let me know what's the most important. Like if they [clients] ask questions sometimes, sometimes they [guides] rearrange the questions so that it's more important to hear the real truth of their answer. It may not even be related to their questions. In that way they're guided to hear something that will click their soul pattern into a change, an awakening."

In other words, when clients come with individual questions, the answers may actually address other matters, unwittingly more important for them to hear.

"I ask them to bring their questions already written out … Mostly it's what they need to know [that comes out]. I think especially for young people that are losing their [way], to see how the soul and the spirit and the mind are all, with different kinds of emotions so we can identify them, and figure out what's going on with us, you know? On the spiritual level."

Serafina has some repeat clients. She does long distance readings but thinks it's nice if the client can be present. She said, as with many things, it all comes in patterns. She is wary, however, of clients who only want you to tell them what they want to hear.

"It just depends, and again, you might have people repeating [visits] that didn't get it. And they go to another intuitive and another intuitive and another intuitive and, in a way, unless you are really seeking the answers to your questions, you're going to go on long journeys. So that's when I ask spirit to 'send me the people we can really help.'"

Although Serafina is in the business of providing intuitive guidance, she ultimately believes if we could each look to ourselves for this, we would all be better off.

"I really think the more people are able to tap in and tune into their own guidance, the better off we'll all be," she said. "It's all spiritual healing."

She warned that, sometimes, a client's own "stuff" may influence an intuitive who is not clear and centered, just as an unfocused intuitive might influence what comes through for a client.

"And the fear one might have is not your fear, it's someone else's, it's their own lesson, their learning. It's their own patterns and behaviors that they need to examine and look at. And they're just caught up in fear, and we lose track of the potential.

"So the angelic hosts are always saying, 'Stay in tune with your Godself, your highest self.' Otherwise, you'll be wiped off the map.'"

In other words, if you portend to bring through guidance from divine levels for others, make certain to keep that connection with your own divinity intact.

Meditation and Communing with Nature

Serafina is not comfortable with the idea of suggesting how a person should meditate.

"I think meditation is very much an individual process, and each person, each soul has their own way of finding it," she said. "Again, I don't think there's one way. Sometimes people can be active and be running and that's when their meditation is. It's finding your bliss, it's finding … what enhances your smile and heart and joy for life. And if it isn't giving you that, then maybe it isn't the right thing to do. Maybe meditation is perfect for some people, and maybe there's something more appropriate for other people."

Her bliss is often found in communing with nature and being in touch with the devic community.

"I have worked a lot with the devic kingdom," Serafina said. "The devic kingdom are the little spirits in the trees and the flowers. That's one of my favorite [places] … I go in the garden and I feel I'm in heaven."

She said sometimes she sees nature spirits, though not always.

"But I've been talking to a certain tree lately," she said. "I know that sounds sort of strange, but this is such a magical kingdom, and, well, it could be. I'm enjoying this area right now. This is very devic … and I never really appreciated it more until I went to Ireland last year and traveled with a most wonderful woman who took me—she was a mythological professor—and we went way back in the early dwellings of the ancients, even before the druids, and I realized how much the devics have been alive all through this whole process of life, you know? And how much the trees and the plants want to talk to us."

Serafina knows there are other people who are in touch with nature as she is, and she thinks more of us might want to consider it.

"I have many people I work with as clients who are in tune and need to be in touch with that [nature] kingdom. There are different realms to connect with, the earth plane and animal kingdom are really talking to us now and helping us awaken to the needs to find balance and harmony and all oneness of life. And we can't ignore where we live. If the water's bad and the pollution and the food, that's the devic kingdom we're corrupting and hurting and harming, and so it's sensitizing ourselves.

"Have you smelled the apple blossoms lately? And have you watched a butterfly? An ant crawling down a tree? The littlest things are the biggest things right now. They all count. They all live on the earth. So I really love living here in this area of Mendocino, in the northwest, because there's so much of the devic consciousness that we're trying to preserve. To be teachers of preserving the beauty of the earth and not irradiate it and fertilize it with chemicals. So I'm a real purist in all the senses!"

And she laughed heartily.

"But that's all part of the devic kingdom and how they're speaking to us. And the animal kingdom, they're trying to talk to us too, very much, they're coming closer to us and closer. If we only opened up more, we can relate and communicate with them … That's just the top of the surface; it's so deep."

Serafina said her interests have mostly been in working with people and the devic kingdom in bringing through information about the wisdom of the angelic realm and in writing inspired poetry and trying to up-level a sense of joy with life.

"We've been pioneers in many ways of going in different countries. And we've been ambassadors for peace in that way."

They have had many adventures along the way. And the way continues.

"Right now I'm working with children," Serafina said, "because I've been guided to do that. I feel the young souls right now are very, very important. They are bringing a great new hope, but yet they are very confused and very frightened—I mean, in the passage of coming in. So their hope needs to be nurtured and protected. Their inspiration's going to be wonderful. So that's what I'm doing a lot now, with children."

She continues to teach ballet, and she paints images of the children in her ballet classes.

"I'm an artist … I'm alone out there in the studio and I was asking spirit, 'Well what am I really doing with this painting?' And they were saying to me, 'You're really doing world healing.'"

And she emits a sweet sound, part giggle, part smile, and very much the child within.

David Cumes

Doctor of Medicine, Diviner of Bones

D avid Cumes is slight in build and strong with a no-nonsense attitude.

At first blush, he is an unlikely person to perform a divinatory practice—surprising even to himself. He is a medical doctor and a surgeon. He once taught at Stanford University. After leaving academia, he established a private practice specializing in urology. He is a divorced father of four.

His former wife, Carol, tricked him a bit into going on a metaphysical journey more than twenty years ago. She signed them up for a two-week trip to Peru in which they would be working with a local shaman, or medicine man. She only told Dave *some* of what the trip was about. Dave was an intense, intelligent, unrelenting skeptic.

On the trip, however, he saw things that surprised him. He witnessed people affected by ceremonies conducted. He saw things neither expected nor quite understood. He had experiences not easily explained by his left-brain self.

Thereafter, Dave became more curious about the metaphysical. Still, there was an abiding reluctance and, always, a stalwart skepticism. In time, his marriage splintered and foundered. With his life spinning in crisis, Dave intensified his spiritual search. He investigated a host of meditative and spiritual practices and possibilities. He delved into

Buddhism, studied Ayurveda, trained in yoga, and eventually returned to his native South Africa to lead groups into the wilderness and to partake of the offerings of local shamans, or "sangomas" as they are called.

Never in his wildest dreams did he expect that one day he himself would advise people by "throwing the bones" to see what the ancestors advised.

Called to The Work

After he began leading groups to South Africa regularly, Dave often consulted with local shamans, or sangomas, about the impending trip. He asked if things would go well or if there would be any unexpected problems, for example. In doing so, sangoma after sangoma told him not only what he asked about, but that *he* was being called to do *their* work. Though wholly unconvinced for a considerable period of time, eventually Dave would return to the bush to study with a chosen sangoma and to learn the divinatory method called throwing the bones.

In throwing the bones, various objects are used, including specific empowered animal bones, tablets hand-carved on one side, or dominoes, common playing dice, stones, coins, or whatever the sangoma is directed to use. Indicators are found in whether the tablets land right-side up or down, the number shown on the die, the prominence of the bones in the way they land, and how the bones fall in relation to each other and the other objects.

Each throw tells a story. Often the die indicates that the sangoma is to throw again. As well as being able to address the matter at hand by studying the lay of the bones, Dave is given information telepathically from an ancestor in spirit whom he works with, which is admittedly strange stuff for a former academic, a medical doctor, and avowed skeptic.

Now his life is not quite his own. "I ... told my daughter," he said, "that when you climb on the wild elephant, you must go where the elephant goes."

Unsuspecting Beginnings

There is a strong tradition in Africa of consulting with native healers or shamans—people who are said to be chosen by the ancestors for the work through a spiritual calling. Frequently, future sangomas are initially reluctant to partake of this kind of work, for it includes ancient and unusual practices, in a now modern world. Some people—Dave among them—believe that the reluctant shamans are the best, because they are not in the work for the power but to provide a service.

Certainly, Dave did not easily accept the notion that *he* should be a sangoma, even though he considers their work valid and useful. Sangomas counsel people, prescribe herbal medicines, diagnose illnesses, provide guidance, and oftentimes work with medical professionals who practice Western medicine. As said earlier, Dave traces the roots of his own journey to that first mysterious trip to Peru, and he credits a midlife crisis of sorts with intensifying his spiritual search.

"Basically the first trip we did to Peru ... I wasn't dragged, [although] I didn't know what I was getting into," Dave said. "It was an interesting trip, and then, of course, I was kind of out of my depth. But I think what really happened was that there was a kind of a midlife crisis, a lot of things happening all at once. One was marital difficulties. Then we moved to Santa Barbara, and that was a really tough time. Going into private practice, transitioning from academics into private practice was hellish for the first two years. And what really happened was I had an existential crisis, so I started doing yoga to try to relieve myself.

"I must say, I'm grateful to Carol for a lot of things, because I think she kind of led the way. Even though it wasn't such fun; nevertheless, she was the one who got me to Peru and probably was the one who interested me in the yoga. And I found I could really get into some sort of a space with the yoga that was really quite compelling, where things didn't seem to worry me as much.

"And then I'd always had this yen to go back to South Africa ... Since I was a medical student, I always wanted to go back and visit the Bushmen, spend time with them in the Kalahari [Desert] ... I'd always thought of it and wanted to do it [and finally] thought, 'Ach, to hell with it, life is short'—and I hadn't been enjoying life too much—'I'll go and spend some time with the Bushmen in the Kalahari.'"

So he did. Dave went first with a group and then arranged for the group's leader to leave him for a month, along with some food and a four-wheel-drive vehicle. He said it was probably a life-changing experience. He had always been intrigued with the wilderness and the Bushmen, and after this extended time in the wilderness, he formulated a theory of using nature as a spiritual practice for transformation. In fact, he eventually wrote a book outlining the theoretical side of his insights. The book is titled *Inner Passages Outer Journeys: Wilderness, Healing, and the Discovery of Self.* He formed a company, Inward Bound, to lead groups into wilderness areas.

"We would just take these groups out, using the principles of what I'd learned from wilderness psychology … about how to get into the wilderness, [in a] more feminine … inner directed way rather than a macho, conquering [way]," Dave explained. "You know, 'bagging peaks and running rapids.' This is the language, the jargon of wilderness, that's very, very confrontational and militaristic, you know … 'conquering a mountain, running a river,' always like that … in regard to … nature."

Because he himself had been quite competitive, Dave understood that attitude of conquering. That part of himself began to bother him, as did conversations that viewed nature as something to overcome, rather than to connect with. He considered it an ego-based notion and non-productive, so he worked first to get his own ego in check and then to keep it there.

"So, in a way, I became a policeman of the ego, and when I did the trips, knowing my own ego so well, I could keep people away from trying to get to the top first … We made it comfortable for them … so they could go into the inner rather than have to worry about survival. And they were very successful [trips]. People had peak experiences and life-transforming things. I structured it the way the book said: the hero's journey, separation, threshold, and then incorporation, which is really what I still do [on trips] … We'll still have those same main structures to work with because they're archetypal and real. You know, they're not theoretical, they're exactly what happens."

Intensifying the Search

While maintaining his medical practice, Dave continued to lead trips to South Africa from time to time. Ever the doctor/healer, he sought healing on some level for the trip participants. Although there were successes, he still wasn't quite satisfied.

"I basically got a bit frustrated because … I was looking for a way to do some alternative healing but with wilderness healing. How often can you do it? … A once-a-year trip is hardly an alternative form of healing."

At that point he intensified his search for other options and explored such offerings as Native American traditions, but none proved to be a sustaining fit. Invariably, he would return to South Africa to lead a small group. Before embarking on each journey, he would ask the locals who the top healer or sangoma in the area was, and he would then check in with that sangoma to see how the trip would go. He would ask whether there would be any problems, for example. By this time, he was a completely different man from the one who first went unwittingly on a metaphysical journey to Peru in 1985.

"Depending on which area I was in, I would always ask, 'Who's the top healer here?' and they would say 'Well, go and see so and so,' Dave recalled. "There were different healers in different areas. Invariably what would happen was … they would throw the bones, and they would say, 'The trip will be fine, but that's not why you're here. You're here because your grandmother's bone, the bones on your mother's side, are calling you to do this work, that you need to do my work.'"

In other words, the sangomas were telling Dave that *he* needed to be a sangoma.

"And you know, the first time this happened [was] in Zimbabwe … and I went to Victoria Falls, and I saw this sangoma, and he just read me, everything. I mean, I was completely blown away," Dave said, laughing lightly at the remembrance of it. "He just had read the whole thing [of my life]. But what amazed me even more, he said, 'You will be doing this kind of work, *my* kind of work.' And I thought, 'Oh that's ridiculous.'

"And then it happened again and again and again and again— different sangomas each time [saying the same thing]. Eventually I started to take it fairly seriously, but I didn't think I had any abilities, you know? I thought … I'm pretty intuitive, but I'm not *psychic*."

Dave couldn't figure out how he could possibly be any good at a divinatory practice if he was not psychic or otherwise able to *see* or know things when the bones are thrown. Though Dave was now open to the metaphysical side of things, he was deeply skeptical about himself as a diviner and about his place in the world of native African healers.

Then he had an experience that was radical enough to alter his view.

"One day I was in the bushveld near the Kruger Park, and we went to the [local] sangoma, and the husband was throwing the bones, and he was about the most pathetic bone thrower I've ever seen," Dave recalled. "He was totally useless. As this just went on, he became less and less impressive, but then … there started to be this shrieking and this noise and this drumming and shrieking in the courtyard. And then he said, 'Ooh, I must stand aside now because there's another spirit who's coming in to talk to you directly.'

"Then this woman came into the room, into the hut, and she was totally out of her gourd, out of her mind. She looked totally possessed, demented, quite frightening, and then all these other women came in and started to drum, and she started to channel. But when you see this kind of channeling, it's completely different; I mean, there's nobody home. There's a spirit in the body, and this woman is completely taken over, shaking and sweating and talking in tongues. She's talking in a different language to her own language.

"Then the husband translated and basically the message was, 'You're ignoring your ancestors. Your migraines won't go away until you listen. You've got pain in your back and that's from your ancestors calling you, and they want you to come back to South Africa and be initiated. And they want you to buy a red cloth and a white cloth' and all these instructions, you know, 'and a cow and a bull and a hut…'"

Dave laughed at the recounting of it. "I was completely overwhelmed by the experience. I mean, it was one of the most powerful experiences I've ever had. I thought, 'Well, you know, this is—it's time to do something.'"

Searching for His Teacher

Dave set out to find someone who might teach him. In his research, he came upon a book titled *Called to Heal: African Shamanic Healers*. It contained stories about African sangomas and how they had been called to the work. The author, a Western woman, wrote about how her son was accurately diagnosed by a sangoma as having an undetected heart defect.

Dave had a friend in Johannesburg who operated a bookstore. Dave asked him to see if he could find out how to contact the author directly.

"Then things just happened serendipitously, you know; it's just the way it works," Dave said. "Her name was Susan Schuster Campbell, and my friend in Johannesburg who ran the bookstore found out where she lived. She lived in Irvine, California! Right down the road. So I called her up one day, and we chatted, and we actually became friends ... and she said, 'Well, there's two of them,' [sangomas] she would recommend. One was in Johannesburg in Soweto, the other one was [named] PH in Swaziland.

"I went to see the one in Johannesburg, and although I liked her a lot—she had been a nurse, and she was westernized, which was an advantage—but I didn't want to do it in an urban setting. I wanted to be out in the bush, closer to the original model.

"So being a doctor and all left brain, I went systematically around trying to interview different people, when one of my other friends who's in the book [by Schuster Campbell], Shado, said, 'You know, your ancestors will tell you where to go; don't worry about it.'"

Dave went to see PH in Swaziland. PH was not convinced that they were not intended to work together.

"He said, 'No, we must throw the bones and see what the ancestors say: if this is right.' ... Basically he didn't look too convinced," Dave recalled. "And he threw the bones and he said, 'No, no, the ancestors say not only must I teach you [about healing], but I must teach you to throw the bones like me.' He was actually one of the best diviners I've ever known of.

"And then he, he sort of laid it out. He said, 'You know, you can't go and get possessed in California, they'll think you're mad, so you have to do it with the bones.'

"And then, I got initiated," Dave said.

Possession of a Sort

As Schuster Campbell explains in the introduction to her book, it is not uncommon in Africa for diviners to allow themselves to be possessed by spirits or ancestors from the spirit world who are not limited by time or space in what they know and see. As she explains it, for these healers, possession is a positive thing and signifies a close link to their God, through these ancestors.

Although one of the standard ways sangomas get information is to be possessed by spirits, Dave's grandfather came to him in a dream at the beginning of his initiation and told him that he would not be physically possessed where he would allow some other spirit to occupy his body. Dave thinks he has too strong of an ego to give way to total possession; plus, he's not so sure he would want to anyway.

"Somebody else ... especially people who've had abuse issues, they can dissociate very easily from the ego. In some instances it's easy for them to move aside so somebody else can come in."

Dave said although a part of him wanted to be possessed initially, because that is the way it is commonly done among African sangomas, he had serious apprehensions.

"That was one of the things that really scared me. You know, I wanted to, because I thought, 'Well I have to do it because it's [part of it],' but on the other hand, I thought, 'Well it's a bit weird, you know, it's not in my culture.'"

PH quickly ascertained that possession was not to be the best course for Dave, since he might well be looked upon as crazy, if he was found doing that type of thing in a place like Santa Barbara, California. Dave admits to being a bit relieved. For him, it was to be possession of another sort, more like companionship.

"Okay, well, what happens, you see, with the initiation is essentially you are possessed and *possessed* is a strong word, but you can be possessed in many ways," Dave explained. "Basically, being possessed means that an ancestor wants to work through you. So the way that it ... worked for me is my grandfather and my uncle—you know you have your own main blood root spirit guides—were the first ones that contacted me, especially the grandfather on my mother's side. And they tell you that you need to do the work, you know? And then when I went to three people, including PH [who] said to me, 'No, there's a black woman that wants to work with you, who will be the guide for the bones.'"

Dave said his ancestors were introducing the black woman to him, because throwing the bones had been her expertise when she was alive, not theirs. He said people who have passed over to the other side have their own areas of expertise, just as they did when they were living.

"So in other words, if I'm dead, I can't suddenly start to come to you and give you business advice, because that's not my skill," Dave explained. "I can come to you and give you medical advice, surgical advice, because this is what I am and what I know.

"So this woman, whose name is Mpofu, was a sangoma when she died [and] when she lived. And she actually worked in my grandfather's home. A lot of people ... in South Africa are domestic servants, but in their spare time ... they're healers, and nobody knows about it because they do it in their own space and their own time.

"*Now* of course they wouldn't care about telling you, because it's now a black country, but in those days [of Apartheid] nobody would tell you such. So essentially, what was told to me and related was, this woman Mpofu had been a sangoma, and now she wanted to work through me. She hadn't completed in her own life what she needed to complete, and now she uses somebody else to complete her destiny. Because, when you go to the other side, basically they ask you two questions: 'Did you remember your promise? Did you fulfill your promise?' If you didn't fulfill your promise completely, then you can do some of it from that side before you come back. You can work diligently, and I guess you earn karmic brownie points by doing that."

Strange as it all was, it was somehow right for him, and Dave became a sangoma. Mpofu and his ancestors help him to interpret the bones and suggest things to him, and he is uncannily accurate when he reads the bones. It was not always this way. At first, he charged people a dollar when he threw the bones for them. He was still being initiated; the dollar showed appreciation to the ancestors as he found his way as a diviner.

Throwing the Bones

Dave said every healer or medicine man or woman has his or her own system of divination. While PH was teaching Dave, he was also teaching his technique to Mpofu, who is always with Dave in spirit.

"I sit with PH and his bones, and she [Mpofu] learns the Morse code of the bones at the same time that I'm learning it. Well, she actually knows it anyway, because she's not localized in space and time, and she's got a knowing, and seeing everything at once, so she can see how PH works. Then PH transmits to me how he works, what his bones mean.

"Each one is a metaphor for a different polarity: husband, wife, children, money coming in, money going out, reverse polarity, sickness, ancestors, witchcraft or no witchcraft, heart, spirit part, life part. All those things are presented in the bones by different animal bones with the right kind of energy in the bones.

"So the energy in the bones is important because it has power. The hyena bone is the thief … that comes in the night; so if you're looking for a lost object … you look at the hyena bone. If you want to look at the ancestors, you look at the lion bone, because the ancestors are the lion. If you want to look at witchcraft, you look at the baboon bone because that represents witchcraft."

Although there are similarities, every sangoma's system of throwing the bones is different. To be most effective, you need to stay with one technique.

"So what really happens is that the fields of intention and energy are set up between me and Mpofu and the client. For instance … when you ask me to throw bones, Mpofu knows. She knows your name, she knows where you stay—she actually knows, because she's with me all the time … Because she's [there] very constantly, that's this idea of being possessed … Now, my ancestors are there 24/7. So Mpofu is there present when I throw the bones; in fact, she throws the bones, and I just read the message. I'm just the messenger."

Reading the bones is like reading the waking dream that is the person's life. Dave said the bones are always accurate, but they are open to interpretation. For instance, if what he says does not feel right to the client, he can twist the metaphor around to find the right interpretation, just as he might with a dream.

"You're [the client] the one who's the final arbitrator of the dream; it has to feel right to you to be true. The same is true with bones. That's very democratic, you know. If you don't agree with the bones then we twist the metaphor around. The metaphor is real, but interpretation varies. So, for instance, money and energy are interchangeable, so it might say you're completely broke, but you may have just won the lottery, so it's … [that] you don't have any energy."

Dave is given information in other ways as well.

"There's another part to it, which is more like channeling, where … you find yourself just saying things that have nothing to do with the bones. And you're not sure where they're coming from. Other guys don't need bones; they're completely psychic. They can just see it. But because of my training and my left-brain orientation, I don't … get visions … Occasionally I'll hear voices. I get sort of gut feelings or buzzing in my ears or hear a voice or get a dream; but mainly the bones are a very systematic, reproducible way of doing it each time, so you don't have to wait to get the vision or whatever."

Dave even throws the bones to see whether or not to take a given person to South Africa with him on an Inward Bound trip. If the bones say no, he simply tells the client that, for whatever reason, the ancestors don't feel it's in their best interest to go at that time.

Basically, the way the bones fall in relation to each other is what his teacher taught him to interpret in regard to the question being asked. Additionally, Dave sometimes gets inspired information, which he has learned to trust. He may also ask to have a dream to help a client with an answer, but he rarely finds it necessary because the bones are so reliable.

"Yeah, sometimes a dream, but it's very accurate [throwing the bones]. I've had people come again and again, and they say, 'Oh, you know, this turned out to be completely true.' It's often about relationships; frequently it's saying, 'No, don't go there,'" Dave said and laughed. "Then, they come back six months later, and they'll say, 'Oh, I wish I would've listened.'

"And they [often] don't listen to the next one either."

Because people have free will, they choose their course of action. Oftentimes, if they don't like what the bones have to say, they choose not to heed what is presented.

Seeking Self-Guidance through the Bones

Dave has learned to throw the bones for himself, although sometimes it's a tricky matter.

"I can, but obviously I have to get beyond my own subjectivity. So if I have a lot of emotional interest in it, it's difficult, because then you're not reading the polarity completely objectively … But usually now I've gotten to the point where I can throw them much more for myself, and a lot of the sangomas will not do that. But PH said, 'No, you must do it.'"

Dave said PH throws the bones for himself all of the time, and he insisted that Dave learn to do likewise. Dave does, but he also considers that his emotions may factor in his reading. As with every intuitive practice, it is often common for diviners to have a difficult time getting information for themselves, for getting beyond their own *stuff* or desires, to *see* objectively is surmounting a great hurdle.

"Also trusting that the message is right," Dave said. "Because what's also happened—I'm learning all the time, so in the early days, I wasn't quite sure even if I was right, even with people who came. That's why in the beginning I didn't used to charge very much. I thought, 'God, how can this be right?'—And it was right!"

"Then, with myself, I would think, 'Well, they're not going to let me read for myself,' but now I know they do. So, it just comes with time and with trust …

"For instance, I had a girlfriend some years back, and they kept saying 'No no no, get rid of her, get rid of her,' in the dreams, in the bones. I didn't, and by keeping her it was actually very educational because I could see exactly all the things they said came to pass. So, sometimes, in a way, I've kind of done my own scientific survey by just honoring the process and then seeing how it turns out and then verifying that, in fact, they're almost always right. In fact, they're always right.

"But you see, free will is rule, so they won't overrule your free will *ever*. In the end of the day it's up to you. They just advise."

How the Bones May Help People

Dave holds fast to his belief in the validity and worth of the guidance offered by the better sangomas, through the bones. In discussing how he thinks these prophetic techniques help people, he said one way is by pointing out the real issue at hand, when the client may be looking in another direction.

"In my practice, and I do it [read bones] in South Africa, and I do it here, but I think what's happened for me in the West is that I've refined my bones to accommodate to a Western paradigm. So I have special bones [and other objects as] symbols for things that maybe wouldn't be applicable to an African environment. They're just so much simpler.

"So, say an African comes to me and, for instance, the manager of the nearby farm came to me for bones. And he came with a specific question for the bones. The bones actually told him, 'That's not the problem; the problem is his wife.' So the whole thing starts to focus around his wife and problems with his wife and his girlfriend and all this, and he's in denial about that, so it highlights something that he knows about, but the bones say, 'Hey, you need to look at this.'

"Or say a kid you have who's troubled but you don't want to believe there's a problem but the bones say, 'Hey, you need to take care of this kid; otherwise, there's going to be serious issues.'

"It's helpful, in that, firstly, if people are in denial, it'll highlight stuff for them that they may have ignored and the ancestors want to get their attention and say, 'Hey listen, wake up here. Otherwise you're going to be in trouble.'"

He said it might be a health issue that the person needs to pay attention to.

Also Dave believes the bones can give guidance to young people who are lacking it, in a society that is often splintered, with families split up or strewn about the globe.

"The younger people then come; you know, they're *lost*," Dave said. "They don't know what they want to do. They're not sure what direction to take. Should they have this partner or not? Should they invest in this business or not? Should they move or not? It's very empowering to have help and advice, because people don't have that anymore.

"I grew up, I had uncles and aunts and people I could go to for advice. Just speaking to them was very very life affirming. Or your mother or your father or this one or that one or friends. You had this whole extended family, all of them with different skills, so if you wanted this [advice], you could go for that.

"Well, that's what ancestors are. They've all got different skills and they can help you. Not only that, but the advantage is that they're not localized in space and time, so they can tell the past, present, future, and tell you what's going on in New York and California at the same time.

"So it's very life affirming and fulfilling to come and say, 'Really, that the last thing you want at the moment now is to buy another house. This is what you need to do … ' And then they go and they do it and they're so happy because they could have so easily got lost.

"So you're helping people, and there's all sorts of ways to help them, with relationships, with money, with health, with children, against witchcraft, and more frequently, with shades," he said.

Shades as Spirits

Shades are frequently referred to in the African healing paradigm. Dave said sometimes shades are spirits who've attached to a living person— earthbound spirits that are getting in the way of that person's energy flow.

A 'shade' is actually quite common. It is an intrusive spirit that attaches to a living person for various reasons. The most common one is an ancestor who is seeking forgiveness for some transgression [such as abuse]. The ancestor seeks to be released from his or her guilt and shame and reincarnate in a less dysfunctional state. The forgiveness helps to make sure that the ancestor will not come back in another life and perpetuate the same issue.

Dave said things come up with clients that they wouldn't even know about without the bones to show them.

"A woman came the other day, and I said, 'What's the story with the grandfather on your father's side, coming up as a shade?' She said, 'He's the one who sexually abused me.'

"So here she is. Things are not really flowing in life for her. She has this spirit of her grandfather attached to her. He's totally mortified, with guilt and shame and remorse, and he can't let go. He's earthbound, and he needs to be forgiven and released and told that it's fine. It's so simple. You just do it with a ritual and that's the end of the story. It's like having your appendix out, and you won. You leave her feeling fine and relieved, and I'm sure now life will open up in different ways for her because the energy field has been blocked by this grandfather hanging around."

Dave's work as a diviner using the bones helps him to identify the shade, and his work as a shaman and healer equips him to help the client to be rid of the shade that is impeding life flow.

From Childhood Dreams of Scary Stuff, to Scary Stuff

As a child, Dave never had any unusual experiences that he recalls, only a penchant for having vivid, if rather frightening dreams.

"I never knew what they quite meant," Dave recalled. "They were often frightening, but I used to dream about lions a lot and snakes a lot, and lions are the ancestors. And snakes can either be the ancestors, depending on the snake, or witchcraft. But I remember having dreams where I was literally walking through fields of snakes at the bottom of a garden—just hundreds of them writhing around. They were not nice dreams. And the lions' dreams were always scary, but I think it was indicating that this is kind of scary stuff anyway. So … it was maybe telling me what was to come.

"One of the servants we had when I was young [in South Africa] was a sangoma. He was really a terrific guy, and I really liked him a lot. I was intrigued by him and what he did. I would sneak into his room, and it would scare the hell out of me," he said and laughed. "There was always something there that drew me …"

Dave said that being a sangoma can include scary stuff because it can be a matter of dealing with forces of good and evil.

"I have people who come and they see the bones and they get very compelled by it … [but] a lot of the people are not about service; they're about power. They want the power. They want the ability to tell people things, [and to] make a measure of money out of it. It's really not about power, it's about service. So if you really are on the [spiritual] path, it's about being very humble about it because, in reality, it has nothing to do with *you*. Without the ancestor you're nothing. So it's not a power trip, it's a service trip."

Dave does sometimes consent to teach others about throwing the bones and working with dreams and herbal medicines. But just as he is careful about the clients he takes on his trips to South Africa, he is careful about whom he agrees to teach. Those who are especially eager to learn are often those he is the least interested in teaching.

"Because that's a power trip," Dave said. "It's not about service. At the end of the day, if you're not helping people, then what's the point? If you're becoming a commodity broker with visceral power, then how are you different to somebody selling a Mercedes? Because somebody who gets a Mercedes gets a lot of pleasure out of that too, to enjoy.

"But if I was to find somebody like that [especially eager to learn to throw the bones], I would run a mile. I wouldn't have anything to do with them in terms of wanting to teach them. But the ones that come in and say, 'You know I'm not really psychic, and I don't think I can do this,' but then they have this amazing dream or … they tell you something special and you say, 'Well this is what's involved,' and they say, 'Well I don't know about this …'

"They're not into the power trip. They're pretty humble. They're not hung up on the ego, because that's where the power comes. The power comes from letting go of your ego, because it has nothing to do with you. So if you really want to be more powerful—it's the same with enlightenment you know—go beyond your ego … Attached to your ego, you stay down. Go beyond your ego and ancestors will come and help you. You start to tell everybody how powerful you are, and they get offended."

There are challenges still.

"When … you start to get into it, then as you climb higher up the enlightenment path, the ego gets more tricky and manipulates you more heavily to try and make you think that you're on the right path when you're not, to make you think that you're going beyond ego, when in fact you just have a more subtle form of ego.

"So what happens with this kind of work is that—there's no light without dark—so when you start to work in the light, then the dark forces come to mess with you. So you start to walk a tricky line between, what dream is this? Is this a dream from my ancestors or is it a dream from a tricky dark imposter, trying to get me off track? It can get quite worrying at times, not to mention that some of these states that you have to go through. The trancing and the dancing and the initiations and the rituals. It can be quite bothering. Not to mention also that I've had a lot of experience with witchcraft at [his property in South Africa]; people try to get to me through witchcraft."

Dave's property in South Africa, where he leads Inward Bound groups, covers three thousand acres. He said it can be easy for neighbors in the area to become jealous that he has so much, while they have so little. So he must guard against that type of negative energy, and he does.

He hastens to add that when he himself first read accounts of witchcraft, of grabs for power and the like, he thought it was all "a bit over the top." He doesn't think so now though.

"But, in fact, it's *not*. You know?"

Dave suspects that the matter of people trying to steal each other's power is an ancient factor of some human's nature.

"That's going on all the time, because, basically, the essence of witchcraft is envy and jealousy and it occurs … clearly. I'm sitting there on my mountain and three thousand acres, and there are people down the mountain that are on subsistence food, so it occurs because of that. But it also occurs on the other [spirit] side, so I have to do protective rituals to make sure that I stay in line with the ancestors."

He is protected by the ancestors anyway. Usually, when something covert is going on, he will get a dream telling him that there's something new coming and that he needs to pay attention.

"Because they'll get you where they can, if they catch you unawares," Dave said. He also has a friend who dreams for him and often conveys valuable messages.

He said some of the shamanic work could be a bit spookier than people usually discuss.

"[Dark forces] hook up, corrupt with you. And then, if you really want to do the work, then … you're almost fighting a battle all the time; you're almost in a battle between the light and the dark. The best example I can give you at a higher level of sophistication is if you've seen *Lord of the Rings* … There's a character there called Gollum that represents the dark side, and he's extremely sinister, but he can be very compellingly convincing, because he's incredibly smart. So they will try to convince you with things, where your weaknesses are. For instance, if you look at Buddha, what did they send in before he got enlightened? Three gorgeous women.

"Most of the guys fall because of women, if you look at the guru saga," Dave said. "Usually the woman will get them, and then that's where they fall out of favor. So that's usually, I think, for the men, the big temptation, because you get powerful in a certain way … I guess women get drawn to you, or maybe they're sent to you, I don't know what. But that of course is a sure way to derail your progress. Or even if you're still doing the work [and get involved with a woman], you won't have quite the same attention or focus that you may have had."

Dave is aware of some shamans and sangomas who try to play both sides, so to speak, to honor both the light and the dark in their ceremonies. They do so to strike and keep a balance between the two; then the dark side does not bother them. Those people are walking a fine line, Dave said, and they are not able to be particularly effective in their work.

"That's the problem that happens with some of them, is that they try to play in both fields, and that doesn't work. They're tricksters, you know? And then what happens is they're listening sometimes to the wrong guidance, which can be self-serving. Then of course their power erodes. In reality they have two choices: You can try and walk the fence between the two and play a little bit on both sides and then, I think, you lack power; or you can get incredibly powerful by going over to the dark side. There's just as much power there as there is on the light side.

"But … what I've seen with some of the sangomas is that … they'll have their ancestors, and they'll be powerful, and then things will come their way that will tempt them. Like somebody will say, 'I'll give you 10,000 rand [South African currency] if you kill that person,' and they say, 'I've really been wanting a car a long time and why should I have to suffer,' and [they're going to get somebody to do it] anyway …' 'Yeah, why not.' And so then they go bump the guy off [through their practice], and of course their ancestors are totally mortified. They say, 'No, we're out of here.' So they do lose the ancestors and then of course the dark side come to him and say, 'Hey, no worries, we'll take care of you; just keep on doing this good work?' And then he gets incredibly powerful, but of course he's taken the wrong turn, and so, that's the thing with the dark, if you lose your ancestors … you'll get other ancestors, but they may not be the ones you want," he said and laughed sardonically, before adding, "If you walk the fine line, then I don't think you ever fully come into the power of either [the light or the dark]."

If the dark side also offers power, why not go there? Dave said the dark side is a "materialistic, vindictive, hateful, evil path" and that, eventually, what you give out will return to you.

"All that karma's going to come back to you big time. You could do something quite innocuous; for instance, at my level, I could … manipulate things in a harmless way, abrogating free will … that has a karmic consequence. And a serious one too.

"There's no free lunch; whatever you do comes back to you … I can't stress that too much because that's the integrity of the work, and I think the problem is that a lot of the people, they like to play in both fields."

Dave believes that some shamans he has known who paid heed to both the light and the dark sides are tricksters who only give the appearance of doing good work. He reflected back on the shaman from his first days in Peru—a man who died when he was fairly young. Who Dave now believes was a trickster. On that shaman's "mesa" of power objects, he always gave representation to both the forces of the light and of the dark. While he did sometimes help people, he never came fully into his power, and he was easily pulled over the line.

"Some of them are fairly harmless; they have a good light. But … the other thing is when you start playing in that field [of courting both sides], you lose your protection from the good guys, and [bad] stuff can happen to you where it would normally not happen. When you get abandoned by your own ancestors, then you're free game."

A good sangoma or shaman does good work, working with good spirits who offer people guidance, direction, protection, and sometimes healing.

His Purpose As a Healer

Dave was asked why he got into shamanism, if there are such difficulties to be faced in guarding against meddlesome forces.

"Well, you know, firstly you don't really understand what it is until you start to get into it," he said. "You don't really understand the full measure of it. Maybe if I knew in retrospect what was involved, maybe I wouldn't have done it. But you actually don't have an option ... It's like, you open the box and then you're on the trip and you can't get out. And you don't want to get out ... I'm happier in it than I would be out of it. You know what I'm saying? There's no going back ...

"The same with the life, you know? You can't go back to an old life. It's progression of your destiny path. You're kind of on your path and you take what comes. Ultimately you want to fulfill your destiny ... We're all here to fulfill a single definitive purpose, and it seems that this is my purpose. It's no longer just to be surgeon; it's not just to be a doctor. That's just something on the way. It's to be a healer. And to be the best that I can ... and I've always been that way. When I did surgery, I wanted to be sure that I was the best one I could be, not just another surgeon. It's just the nature of who you are I guess."

Clearly, Dave is on a journey he did not expect to make, at least not consciously. He is encouraged on the way by seeing that he is of valid assistance to people in his work as a sangoma. In addition to throwing the bones, he uses herbal potions in his work and oftentimes offers protection and healing for his clients with the use of medicinal plants.

Obtaining Useful Information

Dave is not entertained by a discussion of abilities, or of talk regarding being psychic versus being intuitive and the like, for he believes that it all boils down to how we get our information and whether it is useful information. He thinks too often we get hung up on words and descriptions of things, when the bottom line is getting helpful information, not examining how it's done.

"So you say psychic and intuitive and everybody has their way. There's clairvoyance where they see things. There's clairaudience; you hear things. There's clairsentience; you feel things. Then there's the dreamers, the people who dream things, like the Aborigines. Then there are the people who get possessed, the mediums, and the trance-channels. So really, if you think of it … you only get your information direct, or you get it indirect. And you either get it directly by, you see a vision, they project a vision to you, or you hear a voice, they talk in your ear telepathically. Or they come into your body, and they channel. Or you get it metaphorically with dreams or with bones, and that's also very fine. Either way, any way, you're possessed, you know? And that's the problem I had. Look, I'm not psychic. I'm not intuitive. I don't hear voices."

He has little patience for a lot of metaphysical talk. He said on his first trip to Peru, when people described the visions they had in meditations, unless they had a useful message, he didn't see the worth of it.

"I used to sit [on that trip] … and everybody's talking [about what they saw in meditation]. To me it was complete crap, you know? 'Ooh this eagle flew down and came and he stood on his back and we went into the underworld.' Who really cares? I mean, what use is that to you? I was thinking [that] in those days, and I'm still thinking that now. Now, if he says, 'Oh this eagle flew down and he flew into Dave's body and I see that he has an ulcer,' then that's useful.

"But [talking] some kind of spiritual mumbo jumbo that makes somebody feel like they're on a power trip, and it's a projection of their own imagination or their own self-admiration society, that's a bunch of crap. So I just think that what it really has to do with at the end of the day is, is this information useful? Are you helping somebody? Because if you're not, then so what? You might as well just go and be self-absorbed in another way."

Dave is practical. He wants his journey and the efforts he puts forth to be of valid use to himself and to those who avail themselves of his offerings. He affirms and applauds people for finding their own way, but he cautions them to seek messages that are useful and helpful.

"That's the important thing. I think people need to recognize the messages they get and in what way they get them and focus on that … So in terms of [being] psychic, you find the word, there are a hundred words for different people, and how they get information. Each one is valid.

"So this is my way, bones and dreams, plant medicines and the healing songs I get in my dreams," Dave said.

The ancestors may well be the lineage of humanity, accessed from other realms, and divided into the age-old ranks of good, evil, and those who try to walk the fine line between the two until, sooner or later, allegiance must be declared.

Bringing Ancient Practices Needed in the West

Dave sees his as a dual role: as one who brings ancient practices of valid use to the West, where they are needed, and as a person who has trained in, taught, and practices Western medicine.

"So if I was to say, what use is it [referring to his work]?" Dave questioned. "Western medicine, you can't compete with in terms of its ability to fix mechanical problems, but on the psycho-spiritual side, we are not nearly as good. And even the psychologists and psychiatrists are very, very, I would say, limited in what they can do. You know, [having seen what the Peruvian shaman] did for people and the difference [in people] and so on, there are just forces out there that people don't even know about that need to be taken into account and corrected.

"So I think that's my job. I've been told that my job is to take from there [South Africa] to bring to here [the West]. There are a quarter of a million sangomas in South Africa; they don't need another one. And there are plenty of white ones too, and there are plenty of very powerful ones, more powerful than I am. But what I *can* do is I can bring some of that technology here. Good people *are* getting bewitched here, [though] they don't believe in witchcraft. People *are* possessed here, but they don't know that they're possessed, and that's important."

Dave knows very well how strange some of this may seem, for he didn't believe in such things at one time. Now, he hopes to be a bridge to understanding.

"I think at my level—the shamanic societies, of course, they all know about this stuff—but in the medical sphere and the people that I talk to in my lectures and so on, they don't understand this paradigm. And even if they know [about] it, they don't believe it."

Just as he once did not.

Clearly, David Cumes is deeply gratified. His long, sometimes troublesome journey has brought him to a place where he is confident that his work in throwing the bones is needed and valuable. On a personal level, various conflicts within him have been amicably resolved.

Barbara Friedkin

Entertainer and Comedienne, to Medium and Mystic

Barbara Friedkin tends to bound into a room. On this day she is attired in black slacks and a matching blouse, tastefully trimmed in pink lace. Her madly curly blonde hair falls just beneath her shoulders in a bountiful cascade. Her facial features are small and delicate, and she is wearing a stylish pair of eyeglasses.

Her living room is interesting and busy with numerous pieces of art on the walls: prints, paintings, and drawings. The tables are adorned with delicate and interesting objects—treasures discovered in unlikely places such as area thrift stores.

"I'm the psychic shopper!" Barbara announced happily, pointing out various objects such as pottery and prints and their emblems of validity. Most were purchased for a pittance.

"Four dollars!" she exclaimed delightedly, picking up a piece of Frank Lloyd Wright–designed stained glass.

The décor shows a creative flair—feminine and dramatic, much like its occupant.

Yet somehow, it is her dog Wilbur who sets off the room. He is a sleek and elegant whippet that Barbara has had for fourteen years. Once she found him, she decided to name him Marcello, she said (pronounced in a *very* French way), but when he wouldn't respond, she was forced to call him by the name he'd been given: Wilbur. He does not look like a Wilbur. He most certainly could be a Marcello. His black and white coat has fine rows of alternate shadings, and his large eyes are dark and round. There is a sweetness to him. Sleek, graceful, and calm, he is wearing a mink collar.

Barbara, who is in her fifties, was in the entertainment industry in California for many years. It remains her first love. "It's my bliss," she has said. She taught acting, wrote scripts, performed standup comedy routines, and sang professionally with the likes of Dolly Parton (who, Barbara said, once told her, "Girl, you can sing!").

Barbara's psychic abilities evolved in part as a result of her own interest in going to psychics. Also, as a child Barbara was often quite ill and feels she learned then to dissociate herself from the body and enter another dimension in order to escape the pain of the illness. She and girlfriends played psychic games as teenagers and even into adulthood.

In more recent years, after she and a friend got tired of paying to consult with professionals, they decided to practice on each other. Barbara was "off the wall" in her accuracy with things that came through; however, it was mostly *people* who came through—people with names, people who were no longer living.

Barbara has a clear sense of herself, and her place in the world of metaphysics.

"I am not a psychic," she declared, "I'm a medium."

Some say mediums are instruments of the spirit world who can bridge the dimensions.

Working Only through Prayer

Extensive prayers precede all of Barbara's sessions. Working through prayer, Barbara mediates conversations among the living and people who have crossed over to the other side in death. She is remarkable in her ability to bring through a range of people, information, and messages, accurately and often quite unexpectedly.

Although she does not say so, one gets the sense that she learned through experience the folly of making contact without first prefacing it with thorough and complete prayers.

"I prefer getting into a state. I prefer going through prayer," Barbara said. "I prefer going through a process where I'm getting information and writing it down; otherwise I feel like it's just me ... I prefer connecting, because, as a medium, I feel like I'd rather be connecting [spiritually with the other side] first.

"I'm more accurate when ... I prepare myself to communicate," she said.

Barbara believes the prayers she uses provide her with protection from unsavory sources and possibly damaging messages for the clients. Her prayers provide her with protection and guidance.

"Without the prayers I'd be kind of [like], 'Yikes!'" Barbara said.

She is very specific about the spiritual figures she appeals to initially in her prayers.

"In the mid-eighties I had a dream that somebody came to me and healed me in the name of Jesus Christ, which is a little disturbing for a Jewish girl. But they healed me three times in the name of Jesus Christ. I also realized that I needed to work through prayer, and the most important thing for me is that I do pray to Jesus and Mary, and Buddha and Qwan Yin [who Barbara considers the female counterpart of Buddha] primarily, and other people too.

"I think that as you pray to Jesus Christ ... I just ... see him as a great spiritual figure *and* a Jew. So I'm not uncomfortable with the vibration ... He just seems to be at the head of the earthly heavenly realms. And I call on Him ... and Mary and ... Buddha and Qwan Yin. Those are my first four that I get into and I ask [for help from]. I go through a process where it's pulled in a lot."

While in prayer, Barbara asks that any information that comes through for others be beneficial to them.

"The one thing that I do say in my prayers—and this is very important—is that I want information that will make things better for the person that I'm reading for ... It's the power of intention, and if I don't get to that in my prayers, sometimes they won't give me information."

Barbara isn't entirely certain *who* is facilitating the process of her mediumship, but it *does* appear to be guided and orchestrated.

"It's funny, because ... I do get help. People from the other side who are with that person [the client], they'll bring [in other spiritual figures]. Like, I was reading a guy—I thought he was Hispanic, and I'm in my prayer and I'm [saying], 'Thank you, Lord Jesus, thank you for my gift and thank you for allowing me, and may I have permission?' I really go through a whole rigmarole of prayer, and I will get messages [such as], 'You're not ready yet; we're not going to tell you yet.'"

Returning to the matter of the client who she thought might be Hispanic, at the beginning of his session, she had a thought about what might be appropriate for him.

"I start thinking, should I be praying to Our Lady of Guadalupe because I'm thinking that he was Hispanic? But I get interrupted with a name, which was (pronounced) Fatima, and it was his mother who had passed, and they were Arabic. And then she said, 'Don't forget the great prophet Mohammed.' So I wrote this stuff down.

"That's why, while I'm in my prayers, I start writing down what … they start throwing into me, outside of the realm of what I know are my specific prayers … I wrote down Fatima, and it turned out that he was a Muslim."

Barbara is not completely certain whom she is working with from the other side, but sometimes she has a sense that some of her family may be involved in assisting her.

"I just let it go [after praying]," Barbara said. "Sometimes I feel like it could be my grandmother; I feel like it could be my grandfather. I do get a very strong sense of my grandmother, who died when I was young. And a lot of the people who will show up for the other person [client] will just [say], 'I'm here and you can hear me.'

"So I do get a lot of their [clients'] people [in spirit who] will come and help me with the prayers. They'll [say], 'No, you're not ready yet; you haven't thanked the sea creatures yet,' [or] 'You haven't thanked the whales and the dolphins and the seals,' and I have to do that. It's really funny. Or sometimes it'll just start coming up [the information]."

The guidance and information often begin to come in when she is in the prayer state.

"I go through my prayers, and a lot of times, when I'm in my prayers, I'll get, I'll literally hear somebody say or [I'll] cognitively get an understanding that they're saying, 'Not yet' and 'You need to continue.'"

Once her prayers are complete, Barbara is confident that she is protected and will only be in touch with personages that intend to bring through information that is helpful to those present.

"I take whoever shows up [after the prayers are said]. I just am open. It's like you tell me, and that's also why I write things down. In the prayers, I start to receive information, and I just write it down, because … I want to be able to prove it, to be able to say, 'See, I wrote this down.' … I'm a realist and a skeptic."

She questions whether prayer is as much a part of her daily life as it might be. "I should probably pray more and I'll pray if things get strange for me," she said. "But I really work through prayer when I work."

From Pains and Prophetic Dreams, to Voices

Barbara lives in Cave Creek, Arizona, a once dusty mining town that is now a tourist destination and charming enclave in the foothills of the Bradshaw Mountains north of Phoenix. She has a private practice and also sometimes gives public presentations at the local library. These sessions often leave attendees in the audience stunned when the unexpected happens.

In public forums, Barbara works somewhat like John Edward, a well-known medium and author who has had television programs. He sought to connect members of the audience with their loved ones who had crossed over. In fact, one program was called *Crossing Over with John Edward.*

In private sessions, Barbara works much as she does publicly, yet there are differences. Privately, since the identity of the recipient the messages are intended for is known, it is sometimes as if she facilitates conversations between the client and those who have passed over. She passes questions on, and gives answers and likewise relays requests and messages from those in spirit to those among the living. Her work, while sometimes lighthearted and punctuated with laughter, can also be deeply serious, especially when dealing with clients who are grieving.

"Okay, how'd I get into this?" Barbara reiterated, as if reaching to remember. "I think my mother always called me Chicken Little because I was always saying things were going to happen … and they *would* happen. But my mother's phrase was always, 'Well, we'll cross that bridge when we come to it,' because I always anticipating what was going to happen.

"In my hippie-dom I played a lot of games with friends, but I'd already had some advantages because I was very sick. In fourth grade, I was in a coma and I think that taught me."

Barbara believes that she learned to go into altered states as a child so that she could tolerate her illness and allow her body to heal.

"I also had the pains that I couldn't handle, and I think in my sleep I learned how to astral project. I learned how to get out of my body in order to tolerate, so I could finally let my body rest. I was able to consciously let go …

"And I remember that I had a lot of little things [then]; it started to get much more profound."

Barbara said her abilities began and increased with small things. She practiced, in a sense.

"I played games with my girlfriends. I'd pick up the phone and they were there. Before it rang. We would do it. We would consciously try to do that—pick it up before it rang."

In addition to playing psychic games with friends, Barbara had a history of dreams that predicted future events. She jokes lightly about the unfolding of one, although it haunted her for years.

"When I was sixteen, I had a dream that I found my father dead in a bedroom, and it took him until I was forty-six before he actually did it," she said, laughing. "Found him in the bedroom. So, I mean, I'm waiting my whole life: When am I going to find him?

"So it was like, oh my god, do I have to go visit Dad? It was bad enough visiting Dad, but then on top of it, I could find him at any time. And even when it happened, I was shocked."

Barbara often felt a need to consult with psychics, mostly about business or men. During those visits, she was often told that she was psychically gifted. She wasn't particularly interested.

"I started to go to psychics, being in Hollywood where people are messing behind your back all the time, you kind of go, 'What's going on?' and with men [in her life]. A lot of them [psychics] weren't right, but a lot of them would tell me that I had a gift as well."

Though many of the psychics she visited were often wrong about the information they gave Barbara, she noticed that she was consistently being advised that *she* was psychically gifted. Yet she remained largely ambivalent about those abilities.

"They would say, 'You've got certain psychic abilities,' but they didn't necessarily [get specific] … It was nothing I was [that interested in]. I was pursuing the entertainment business … I had written a rock musical in the seventies. I moved to Los Angeles, but I was still pursuing the musical at the time in different venues and so forth … It had run in San Francisco.

"I'd say the things that really started happening strongly for me were in the early eighties."

Barbara recounts one of the first incidents that made her begin to pay serious attention to her clairaudient guidance.

"I was in New York in 1983 for my thirtieth birthday, and I kept hearing, 'Go to Bloomingdale's,' and I responded, 'I don't want to go to Bloomingdale's.' It was in 1983 and I said, 'I don't like what they have; it's all preppy stuff.' The voice kept telling me, 'Go to Bloomingdale's.' And this was one of the first times—very significant story because it very much … wasn't the dream state. I was wide awake and hearing the voices and listening to the voices. In fact the voices would *not stop* making me listen to them to go to Bloomingdale's. I'm arguing, 'I don't want to go to Bloomingdale's; I don't like the clothes.' 'Go to Bloomingdale's,' I would still hear.

"Finally, I just get on the subway, I go down, and I'm sitting on the subway, and I'm going [to other passengers], 'Fifty-eighth street to go to Bloomingdale's, right?' So I get off the subway. I go upstairs [at Bloomingdale's], and I heard five voices singing a cappella do-wop, and I start to turn the other way, and I hear the voice literally say to me, 'What are you, some snob from LA? These people are good; go see them.' It was like, okay. So I went up, at the very last note. They're standing up on the mezzanine, and at the top of the stairs is one of the absolute loves of my life, Frank, who I got split from because they took him … on tour."

The two had met in Chicago and planned to attend San Francisco State together. Barbara did, but Frank, a singer, was hired for a musical and taken away on tour. He ended up starring on Broadway in a show.

"Even though I'd seen him over the years, I don't think I'd ever resolved my feelings ... and there he was. And we spent two days hanging out together ... and we resolved the relationship.

"So I was sent there so I could move on. I was very clear about that the second day, and I actually moved on and got involved with Greg, but that relationship was hanging me up for ten years. And I didn't even realize that it was hanging me up for ten years, but there it was, and that's when the clarity of the voices became very apparent to me, that it wasn't that I was crazy, but I was actually getting information."

A Spirit Whispers in Her Ear

Barbara left New York, returned to California, and soon had an experience that shook her to her core.

"I go back to my life in Hollywood. I get hired by Bette Midler to perform character for her private parties as a character named Linda Thompson. I did that for a number of years. And over the time period ... I moved again up to the Hollywood Hills, and I had a *very* profound experience when I was sleeping, where I was asleep on a hot afternoon, and I had a dream that I was literally, with my arms out, literally, like I was tied to a cross, though I hate to say it and I [usually] don't—I'm not into that per se—but I was out, my arms are over a swimming pool.

"And out of the corner of my eye, I see a woman who looks like she's asleep in a black bathing suit and there's two little girls. One's in a polka dot bathing suit. One's on a diving board, and the other's in the pool. The one in the pool is drowning, and the other one tries to help her and falls in. I watch the first one drown. I'm in a panic. I can't move.

"I see a white light, a stream of white light leave her body, go through my heart, fourth chakra, and out of me. I'm just *horrified*. The second one, the same thing, she drowned. I think she really wanted to follow her sister; she was determined to stay with her sister, and she may have been able to save herself, but there wasn't even a thought of it. And a *longer* white light came out of her and came through my heart.

I'm just horrified at experiencing this scene. Into my right ear I feel the spirit of the older girl come into my ear, my right ear, and say to me, 'We're at peace.' I had the overwhelming sense of peace.

"I woke up ...

"I turned on the television at five o'clock that afternoon, and Kelly Lane was the newscaster ... and she announced that two little girls in Beverly Hills, at the time I was having this dream, had drowned in a swimming pool and that their mother was there and was, you know, unable [to help]—I'm not sure what the details were ... But that confirmed to me that that's what I saw."

That experience has stayed with Barbara. Sometimes she tells the story to others, especially those who have lost children. Sometimes it demands to be told, and then she will find that someone in the audience has lost a child. The experience taught Barbara that those who cross over to the other side are generally fine; in fact, they are often more at peace there than they ever were here.

While the experience of watching the two girls drown and pass into spirit was deeply profound for Barbara, it would still be some time before she would take her gifts seriously.

A Mysterious Stranger's Pronouncement

Up until the early nineties, Barbara was still all about LA, the entertainment industry, and living the life. Then an earthquake struck.

"A nice big Whittier shaker," she recalled.

Even though she had predicted the earthquake to a friend, it frightened her. She carried on in LA for a while longer, and then a long hot summer arrived, and with it a writers' strike. Those events conspired with another earthquake to send Barbara scurrying to Arizona to visit family. She was still shaken from the earthquake, so her cousin suggested she go up to the charming town of Cave Creek, just to get away.

"And I went into a little place that used to be here in Frontier Town [a local shopping center] called The Rock Shop, and I'm walking around looking at the different rocks, and there's a man in a dusty outfit. It was gray. He was missing some of his teeth. His hair was kind of ratty and matted, and he was kind of dusty and dirty. He's walking around with me in this little shop, and he's telling me which rocks are which. 'Oh, that's azurite and this is amethyst,' and he's just describing [the rocks] … He's pointing out to me what the rocks were and where they were from."

Arizona is a heavily mineralized state, and Cave Creek was established as a mining town.

"He knew all about the rocks," Barbara said, continuing. "And he started asking me about myself …

"So he looked at me and he said, 'You belong here.' And I said, 'Oh my god, in this dusty, dirty, little town? Or in Arizona *at all*?' I said, 'Oh my god, I hate Arizona.' And he said, 'No, you belong here.' And I said, 'Oh my god, I'm a comedy writer from LA!' in my best valley girl [affectation] …"

With a valley girl nuance, she mimicked herself. 'Oh my god! I'm a comedy writer from LA!" she said, and shook her hair as if to recount the experience of fending off the notion of something so absurd as living in Cave Creek.

Then, resuming her normal tone of voice, she continued the story.

"He said, 'No you're not. You're the Mystic of Cave Creek.'"

She resumes the valley girl affectation and tosses her blonde hair about, "'Okay, oh my god.' So I kind of walked away from him and brought my stuff up to the counter, and I talked to the woman at the counter and said, 'Oh, that guy was kind of weird,' and she said, 'What guy?' And I said, 'The guy who was, like, following me around the store.' And she said, 'I didn't see anybody else in the store, I'm sorry.'"

Barbara filed the experience away, but she did not forget it. In the interim, between 1987 and 1994, she did appreciate the fact that she sometimes heard valid information and that her psychic abilities were increasing.

"It [her psychic/intuitive ability] started to develop so profoundly … [Before] I finally moved here from LA, I met a friend who was a newscaster … and we would go get our nails done. She was a beauty queen, and she was Miss Oregon for the Miss USA contest, younger than me but we got along, and we were kind of obsessed with eating sushi. Next to this sushi place there was this psychic guide store, and we'd go in and we'd compare notes [from the readings], and we got more and more interested, and we finally said, 'You know, why are we spending money? Let's read each other.' And I was off the wall when I started reading. She said, 'Oh my god, that's my grandfather's name!' and ... I realized I really did have a very specific gift."

Cave Creek or Bust

It seemed as if events conspired to get Barbara to Cave Creek. Her life in the LA area began to unravel. Agents were lost, lawsuits filed, and life generally spun into disarray. Then another earthquake struck, just as Barbara said it would.

"The earthquake, I predicted ... I put dishes away in boxes," she said, laughing. "I got things off the wall, and there it was ... About two days after the earthquake, I got a call from my Uncle Norman, may he rest in peace, and [cousin] Peter and they said, 'When are you coming out to Arizona?' I said, 'As soon as possible, and this time I'm flying.'

"So I flew out and I went up to Cave Creek again. I went into the school. Within a minute they gave me an artist-in-residency [position] at the Desert Foothills Theatre. I also got a part-time teaching job, and I got a job at a little shop up here."

Barbara likes to tell the story of how that job came about.

"I walked into the shop and I said, 'I'm psychic, give me a pen and a piece of paper, I'm going to write some.' They said 'Show us!' And I read everybody in the room, very specifically. I said, 'There's a bald guy who's Hawaiian, you're in Hawaii with him, and you two are not getting along.' That was her husband. I read somebody else, and I said there's a guy who you're seeing, but I don't know if you know this, but this guy's actually engaged to somebody else to get married, and he's engaged to you too. She said, 'I just found out.'

"I was *right on.* And then I said to this other one: 'There's somebody who's in Europe, they're in Italy, and they're an architect,' and she said my son's studying architecture in Italy. And this man walks in, named Frank, and ... he said, 'Well, read me' and I said, 'Well I don't mean to be repetitive, maybe I'm still picking up on her, but they're talking about architecture around you too.' And [it turns out] he's an architect.

"So, I got my stuff [from California], cried my eyes out, packed up, left, left my friends, everything, and the shame and death of it all, and moved to Arizona where I would [be] reading kind of part-time. I didn't want to make a big deal out of it, because I actually did do a wonderful show with lovely reviews with the kids, and I was also teaching. I taught at the Foothills Academy and I was reading people …

"I … finally made a commitment."

The Mystic of Cave Creek

Clearly, things quickly fell into place for Barbara in Cave Creek. It seems she was to become the mystic of Cave Creek after all. She gave readings part-time, albeit quietly, since she was also teaching young people in the area and didn't want to make a big deal of the mystical side of her life. Although she was increasingly accepting of her gifts, she surprised even herself, because of the dead people who began to come through during her psychic sessions.

"When I got here, there was one reading that really kind of changed my life, as far as knowing that I was getting [good as a medium], and it was a woman who came to me who had never seen a psychic or a medium at all, ever. She came into the store, and I said, 'Come on outside. I'll sit down. I'll read you.' —Slow, hot, Arizona.

"She wanted to know about her trip to Oregon. I said, 'Well that's not how I work,' but I gave her some road advice: Get a cell phone, get a car charger [other safety measures] … 'But here's what I'm getting. I'm getting a bad childhood.' She said—she was with a friend—and she said, 'No, my childhood was fine,' and I said, 'Well, I'm getting the name Steven and I'm getting a very bad childhood.' She said, 'I don't know a Steven and my childhood was boring. I didn't get a lot of affection, but it wasn't abusive.'

"And I said, 'Well this is very abusive. I don't know if you're forgetting something, but let me go on.' I said, 'You've got two sons,' and she said, 'Yes I do,' and I said, 'The oldest one's married,' and I put my fists together and I banged them together and I said, 'He's butting heads with his wife; he's fighting with his wife, and the younger one has emotional problems too.' She said yes they're both having problems, and I said, 'Your husband is nowhere to be found; their father is not in the picture. It's almost like you weren't married to him,' and she said, 'Yes, I don't talk to him. I don't have anything to do with him.'

"I said, 'Well I'm still getting—they're showing me a black heart and the name Stevie and a really bad childhood' and she said, 'Oh, you mean my nephew Steven who killed himself when he was ten?' So I said, 'That's him.'

"That really changed my life," Barbara said.

Barbara did the reading for free, to pass the time on a hot, slow, Arizona summer day, though perhaps the gift of it was mostly to herself and others who would come to her as clients. It changed her life and the way she worked.

Barbara soon moved on to a full-time position in a metaphysical shop in Scottsdale and became the number one requested psychic medium there.

"Practice makes perfect, and I just kept getting very specific information. I hear it, I write it down, and I tell it back to them."

Barbara stayed at that job for a year. While the practice helped her, it was not an environment she wished to continue in.

Learning How She Likes to Work

Barbara credits another psychic, one well known in the greater Phoenix area, with being a mentor. Jan Ross was a kind and giving woman who worked through prayer. Barbara remembered when they first met.

"In '94 when I came out the second time to visit my cousin, he sent me to a woman named Jan Ross. Jan Ross is a very well known ... psychic medium, and she looked at me and said, 'You do what I do. And you can do it. You *really* can do it.' I did weekends in her shop [Jan Ross Gifts & Books], and I got quite a nice response, and she was very nice because she let you read on weekends and then you take your clients home with you. And some places, other places ... it was, 'Sign this. You can't take any clients. Everything comes to me ...'

"But Jan let me [take clients] and offered me things, you know, TV shows [saying], 'They need somebody to do this or that.' So she was very nice about letting these things happen."

Barbara credits Jan Ross with being her adviser and with helping her learn to work more effectively and more completely through prayer.

"Jan Ross, who is sort of a mentor of mine ... was encouraging me to do the psychic work ... She was really, really encouraging, and she said to me a prayer that I do use. This one specific line I do use, and it does help me. It calms me down in all sorts of situations …

"I really go with my instincts. I'm open, and I'll just get the wildest things, and I just write it down."

Training Her Clients to Work with Her

Once Barbara learned how she liked to work, she had to train her clients to cooperate accordingly.

"I got very frustrated with people," she recalled. "If I started saying something and came up with a name and I hadn't written things down, it was frustrating because they started saying things, and it was like, 'I don't want to hear anything!' One of the things I have as a psychic medium is, 'Don't ask me questions. I don't want your questions until *way* after. I don't even want to know your name if I don't have to.'"

She said her clients were frustrating because she wanted to get clear first and go with the information that came, and they tended to jump in with their own information or questions.

"I finally had this girl come to me, she brought a shirt, a plaid shirt [with her] … and I said, 'Don't talk to me; I'm writing this stuff down.' And I wrote it all down and then I read it to her … He [the shirt's owner] was from San Francisco. He was an architect. He was her boyfriend. He had died of a head injury—actually it was a brain embolism, so on and so forth …

"She called me years later [and said], 'You got everything right except you wrote down that I would meet somebody when I was thirty-five, and I didn't meet him until I was thirty-eight.' But if you look at five and eight they almost look the same …

"So that was … what made me write these things down, because I don't want to get front loaded. I don't want anybody telling me anything about them."

Joys and Limits in Giving Readings

Barbara was asked if doing the work tires her.

"It can be exhausting, and one of the reasons I left that [Scottsdale] place was it was psychic abuse; you were under a boss. And a lot of the people, they read cards. They really didn't get into this kind of energy. I did a group reading there once a month, and then I'd do their psychic showcase, and I was their number one repeat psychic. This woman was making a lot of money off of me ... It was *truly* exhausting and a very unhealthy environment, so I really felt I had to get out of there, and I was lucky enough ... [that] the library offered me this."

Public Demonstrations Bring Surprise and Pleasure

Barbara was rather surprised when someone from the local library [in Cave Creek] talked to her about offering her services in a public forum there, but she was very pleased. She said a woman who works for the library approached her.

"[She] came to me and said, 'I know you do this, and I'm with the library and do you want to come up?' I did the first program there, and I ... blew everybody away, and I was getting everybody's everything, names, and who's this person ... And so, here I am today."

Most people are drawn to the event at the library by public notices posted around town or in the local newspaper. The notices proclaim the following:

Connecting with Barbara
Come enjoy a special time of connecting with your loved ones.
Barbara Friedkin,
the Mystic of Cave Creek,
works through prayer to bring needed messages from your loved ones who have "crossed over," giving you the love and information that will heal your soul by gaining closure. Many people also gain insight to unresolved issues and receive information about upcoming events in their lives.
Donations accepted.

On a given Saturday the audience was small. Barbara came into the meeting room as two women were sharing details of whom they hoped to connect with. She held up her hand, quickly shushing them. "Don't say anything!" she demanded cheerfully. "I don't want to know anything."

She prepared the table at the front of the room. She lighted some incense and then briefly explained that she did a form of automatic writing that begins with prayer. She asked the audience to uncross their arms and to pray as she did. She asked them to pray for her, for themselves, and for anyone they might hope to connect with that day. Two yellow legal pads and several ink pens were on the table in front of Barbara. Those present were quiet, with bowed heads, until they heard Barbara begin to scribble. She spoke, and it was clear the prayer session was over.

"They made me go back in [to prayer]," she said, as the audience looked up. "They said," and here she adopted a sing-songy voice, 'You didn't give thanks for your gifts.'"

Barbara continued speaking, but in a different vein.

"I'm getting a grandmother and singing in the choir. She took someone every winter to an event. And I'm getting a grandfather. It was like the grandfather sang in the choir," Barbara said, while scribbling round and round on the pad in what seemed a nonsensical manner.

After a brief silence, a woman in the audience hesitantly offered, "My grandmother took me to an event every year at Christmas. There was the Ice Capades. And there was a choir."

"Did your grandfather sing?" Barbara asked. "Did he sing in the choir?"

"Yes," the woman answered tentatively. "He sang in the Mormon Tabernacle Choir."

"I knew it!" Barbara said, excitedly, delightedly. "Come and look what I wrote!" And Barbara held up the legal pad and pointed to the top of the page where she had written *MTC*.

"They would *not* shut up!" Barbara enthused. "They said, 'It's the Mormon Tabernacle Choir!'" and then she did an impressive routine of singing a rousing round of Hallelujahs.

"They showed me the snow," she said, pleased. "Did she ever call you darling, your grandmother?" Barbara asked.

"Her daughter, which was my mom, did, and she probably got it from her mom," the lady said.

"She's around you and she's been watching you. There's a lot of love here. This was a good family. Big influence …

"Do you teach?" Barbara asked.

"No," the woman said, "My mom was a teacher."

"She's acknowledging that," Barbara said. "You might want to tell your mom.

"You've kind of gotten rid of the Mormon stuff, and she said it's okay. She just wants you to have faith and believe in Christ. Not to do with the Mormons; some of that she's not buying now either."

Some in the audience chuckled lightly and Barbara added, "Sometimes they see things different when they get to the other side.

"There's a question about somebody else," Barbara said to the woman in the audience. "A man? Was there a man that you loved?"

The lady confirmed it.

"He's there too," Barbara said. "There's a shy feeling around him. He's very quiet. He's here though. Would he be sorry?"

The woman said, "He might, but he shouldn't."

Then, through an exchange between them, Barbara ascertained that this would be the woman's father, who had died that year.

"That's the marriage then!" Barbara said, putting the pieces together for herself, if nothing else. "He's dad. There's the feeling of being sorry; it might be to your mother. Did he have cancer?"

"Yes," the woman said and if she was surprised, it didn't show.

"He loves you, but he never told you enough."

"Yes, but I knew it," the woman said firmly. "He wasn't verbal, but he showed it in other ways."

"He took care of you and he loved you," Barbara said. "Do you have a sister?"

"Yes."

"Who was the tomboy?"

"I was."

"So, he's referring to you ... You did the boy stuff, you went fishing, you played ball with him. Did you play ball with him?"

"Yes," the woman confirmed. "He didn't have a son, so I was his son. I did those things."

"You loved this," Barbara said. "He's remembering all of that. He loves you very much."

The woman shifted in her chair, as if letting loose a bit.

"Your father's proud of you," Barbara said. "Are you in the medical field?"

"No," the woman said, "I'm an engineer."

"Are you an electrical engineer?" Barbara asked without hesitation.

"Yes."

"He's very proud of you. You're the most successful one in the family."

"Yes," the woman quietly confirmed.

"'Anyone would be proud to have a son like you,' he's saying," and the people in the audience laughed. "You did it with an unobstructed male path, and you're independent too."

The woman acknowledged it as so.

"Coming from the Mormons, that's pretty good," Barbara said, and again the audience laughed lightly. Then Barbara added, "He's saying that they were liberal Mormons."

People in the audience uniformly smiled.

"Were you wondering about your father?" Barbara asked the woman.

"Yes," she answered.

"He's fine. He's not sick anymore. He was so sick. It was a relief. But not for your mother. It's ripping her heart out not to be with him. They were like twin souls together. He's fine and dandy and not to worry. You might want to tell your mother some of this," Barbara said, and those present fell silent, as if wondering about doing such a thing.

(The woman later reported that no one, not even her husband, knew she was going to see Barbara at the library that day and that she had come specifically in hopes of connecting with her father.)

Later in the library session, Barbara moved on.

"I'm getting a P name," she said. "Someone with a P name who passed over from cancer, pancreatic cancer?" A stunned woman in the audience spoke, saying that she had come in hopes of making contact with Peter, who died of pancreatic cancer six months previously.

And so it went.

Fun with the Work, with Limits

Barbara feels limited in how many readings she can comfortably do on any given day.

"I'd say two a day," Barbara said, "because when I do a reading privately [it takes more effort]. When I would do it in the store, I had eight to ten people, and they just booked me [solid]. I was there from nine o'clock in the morning till nine o'clock at night … for five days. I was exhausted, gaining weight, no breaks. It was worse than working telemarketing—it was like telemarketing to God!" she said laughing, ever the comic.

Barbara said sometimes people ask her to tell them about their past lives, but she isn't particularly comfortable doing so. After all, she mused, how does she know she isn't just making it up? This is not her area of expertise.

"As for past lives," she said, "how can you prove it? I believe in past lives, but *I* don't necessarily want to do it. People ask me about it. If it [a past life] comes up without them asking about it, I will tell them, [thinking] this is interesting because I don't usually get this. If it comes up, I'll put it out there, but what I want—the most important thing—is called *proof*."

She likes the work.

"I have to say, it's fun. And I really like doing it in large groups. I love the entertainment, because I did have the background as a comedienne and a writer and an entertainer, and using both talents [entertainment and mediumship] to help people, and to heal people. People in groups like to heal people … I like integrating my ability to do both, entertain and use it [mediumship]."

She is a regularly scheduled speaker at a national reunion of people who are twins or multiples and always looks forward to it.

A Background Open to Other Possibilities

In addition to her own personal experiences, Barbara came from a family that was somewhat open to the idea of psychics and the like. To help put it in context, she reflected back on a time shortly after she moved to Cave Creek.

"So, at that point, I'm reading and teaching and then my parents died, a month apart, while I was with them. And they were very open to this too … My mother always told me a story. She lost a pregnancy in the womb, and my grandmother said to her, 'Don't worry Mickie, you'll have another child.' And I found out also that my Uncle Norman, my mother's brother, had been going to see [the psychic] Jan Ross … and that's how I got [to] Jan Ross. And my grandmother, who went to Haiti and Cuba off and on … went to psychics. So this was something [in the family]."

Barbara was asked if her mother went to psychics.

"Not my mother," Barbara said. "She went to temple. So the thing that was very interesting, she knew what I was doing after her surgery, before she passed away. And my father passed before her and promised that he'd go first."

Barbara never gave her mother a reading.

"No, no, no. She gave *me* readings; she'd tell *me* what to do," Barbara said, laughing at the idea of a daughter advising her Jewish mother. "I don't tell my mother what to do! But she came out of the surgery, and when they were rolling her into the room … the first thing out of her mouth was, 'I saw Grandma Minga [on the other side], which was our nickname for her mother, Jane … She said, 'I saw Aunt Tet,' who's Aunt Esther, and 'Myrtle was there, but I'm not talking to her.' And my father and I were, like, 'You're *still* not talking to Aunt Myrtle?'

"And then she took a turn for the worst. My father, who had promised that he'd go first, was very upset, and when she went on the breathing tubes, he went home. I woke up in the morning to wake him up to go to the hospital; he was dead. He promised her he'd go first, he always kept his promise, fifty-seven years he kept his promises to my mother.

"They were inseparable and then she went [passed over] a month later. And I know she went [over] with him. Because obviously, it wasn't enough to see her mother and her aunt to get her to cross over, but seeing my dad, she went. And I told her while she was really kind of in and out of it, if you see Dad, go with him," and Barbara laughed lightly.

"But we never told her. He never got to suffer her death, and I never told her that he was dead. Never. So they never had to suffer that horrific feeling of he's gone, you know?

"So, *I* did. I had to suffer, after I suffered with them …

"But in the meantime, I came back, had some health issues, and finally made a commitment. I went into a little shop in Scottsdale and worked there for a year, nine months [actually], and I was the number one medium."

Perhaps knowing that her parents were on the other side had something to do with activating Barbara's own interest in contacting it.

Her Sense of the Other Side

"My greatest sense with this is after we pass, we don't leave, and I know that it's very peaceful, like everybody seems to say, from the girls, the little girls [seen in the vision over the swimming pool]. But I also feel like there are things that are very helpful, like people [in spirit] are around, people to help them. I had somebody tell me that their mom came [to them in spirit] and said, 'I'm here but I'm not helping you; I'm helping one of the other kids.'

"You know what? For me it's just an exercise in faith, because I just write down what I hear and if it belongs to them—and it seems to belong to them, I don't seem to [make it up]. I seem to be very accurate. I seem to be gifted with the ability to [mediate between the living and the dead]—and they're allowing me to hear this, but I also, as I said before, I *can* sing. I can't draw a picture or paint, but I *can* sing well, and I write comedy well, and I can do *this* [mediumship] well."

"I don't necessarily [think everyone can do this]," Barbara said, although she feels we are all psychic. "And when people say, 'You can do this; everybody's psychic.' Well, everybody can sing too, but not everybody can sing well. And I think this is my gift, because, obviously it is."

A gift at last embraced and shared—and done well.

Jenny Ellen Galloway
Windblown Prairies, a Secret Life, Spiritual Heights

J enny Ellen Galloway lives a somewhat secretive life on untamed
   acreage in a sparsely populated state. She writes books, teaches classes,
   and gives intuitive readings, but she wishes to remain anonymous
here, using the moniker of Jenny Ellen Galloway. It allows her to speak
more freely, she said, and keeps members of the church from knowing
just what she's up to, in the rolling hills outside of her town.

Jenny Ellen is a powerhouse of metaphysical information and a
quiet example of living a God-centered life with such certainty that
there's an ease to it.

She is rarely seen rattled. She strategizes, using the energies, her
sense of things, and her guidance, and if she still doesn't know which
way to go, she may leave it to sort itself out, trusting that a missing
element will reveal itself. Upsets, if they come at all, are brief. There is
an ease to her life, an acceptance; going with the flow is part and parcel.
She talks to God. She asks. She trusts. And she listens.

Maybe it is her eighty-something years of living. Maybe it was
raising six kids on the windblown plains of Canada. Perhaps it was
being married for fifteen years before her husband knew about the
hidden aspects of her life. Perhaps it was a series of intense, mystical
experiences. Maybe it is the quality of non-attachment, seemingly

mastered. Perhaps it's her close, almost casual relationship with God. Maybe it's her sweet sense of gratitude, which bubbles up still, in thanks for modest things she's had for years.

Perhaps it's spiritual heights reached, such as times when she heard celestial music. Yet she returns so easily to an appreciation of simple things: a good story, a blooming plant, a humorous exchange.

She's never had a cola. Not a Coke, not a Pepsi. Not once.

"I just seemed to know I wasn't supposed to," she said.

Coffee is out of the question. Her high sensitivity would not abide it. Even a tea bag is dipped only once, maybe twice.

Mystically, she's an unsung hero, which suits her just fine.

"There's an energy in my astrology chart that talks about how I can easily live a secret life," Jenny Ellen said.

A Prayerful Life as a Child

Jenny Ellen believes the single thing that was most responsible for leading her to the work she now does was having a prayerful life as a child.

"I think that's how I first began to develop," she said. "As a little kid, I would talk to God. And then I would listen."

There was a situation in her early home life that Jenny felt needed to be remedied, and she turned to God.

"I was into prayer a lot. And I still feel that prayer is one of the best ways that a person can open to this, because prayer is an altered state of consciousness. I really think that was the big developer for me. I'd be asking for something, and then I'd really listen: 'Well, how 'bout it? I've asked for this, how 'bout it?' And sometimes didn't get answers right then, and sometimes did! So, [it's] staying in that prayer energy.

"God was and is very real to me. I don't ever remember not knowing about God."

Jenny said if she asked for something and God impressed upon her that it was not to be, reasons were not given, it was simply a sense of "that's how it is."

Sometimes, though, she heard what she felt to be the voice of God. She ponders before saying what God sounds like.

"How it would come through is with a note of authority, like, 'This is what it is.' Gentle. Strong. Note of authority. It would be more like God impressing the words in my head. So it wasn't that it was voice as such, but it felt very different from my own thoughts. I believe it's like we have a sounding board in our heads, and messages can come, and then translate."

Jenny said, in years past, she conducted metaphysical experiments with others. Each person asked the same question of God and got the same answer, but in different words.

"It comes in our own language," she explained, "the words we're more inclined to use. That's why you can talk to animals that way. Not necessarily that your animals speak English, but however they comprehend things hits your sounding board and translates into your language.

"That's why I think if a person was well developed in this, you could converse with people in other languages, because those thought-forms would translate into your own language."

A Gifted Child

As a child, Jenny Ellen's mother was aware that Jenny had unusual abilities. Jenny was good at finding lost things, for instance. She would just feel in her body where the item was, would go there, and there it would be.

"Of course, people didn't talk about those things back then," Jenny said. "My mother *did* accept that I had these things."

Jenny thought back to some early examples of being intuitive, unbidden.

"One time my brother was going to date a gal and I just yelled at him and said, 'Don't you date her!' My brother was a lot older [than I] and rather mean, and for me to say something like that was totally not a good idea. But he understood something was wrong. I said, 'I don't know what's wrong.' And he said, 'Well, I'll keep this date, but I won't make anymore.' Then we found out there were some really bad things going on with this woman, just really bad."

At one point Jenny said her mother tried to figure out how it was that Jenny knew things that others didn't.

"And finally [her mother] said, 'Well, you know, you just don't know how you know.' And I said, 'No, I don't.' So there were some times when I was in high school when I would tell her things, and she understood then that I didn't know how I knew and didn't really know any more than what I said. And it's like she respected that."

As a child, Jenny Ellen loved what she still loves: exploring energies, where they come from, and how they can be used. She has conducted metaphysical research for years, mapping the energetic centers of the body and determining how they and their energies can be utilized. Some of her work harkens back to the early Tibetans and what they once explored in their myriad of monasteries and among their solitary holy men.

As a child, she played with energetic possibilities—with unusual successes.

"I think the biggest thing with childhood was loving to feel the different energies in my body. And figuring out what you could do with them. This one could bring a lot of strength, and another one was a good prayer energy …

"First one that comes [to mind] is realizing that I could send a certain energy to chickens, and it would just tame them, and they would pull in and be still, and I could pick them up. They were totally tame to me. And I could do that with little kittens that were wild, or cats. And then I found out I could send it to crabby school teachers …

"I realized later—when I got into this stuff—that it was heart chakra energy. It was just interesting to know that you could feel something and send it."

One might also say that it was interesting that such a thing should even occur to her, and she agrees.

"I know now that either some memory was awakened or the guides on the other side put the thought in me. I think I had done it other lives, so it was easy for them to put the thought in."

Reincarnation Comes Calling

As with most people reared in Western society, reincarnation was not part of Jenny's early belief system. An acceptance of it did *not* come easily to her.

"That was very, very difficult for me to really believe that way," Jenny said. "It was after I had a lot of past life experiences. I just kept trying to interpret them some other way. It's like, a person can have an attitude about something, and ... one's attitudes can be like walls and just literally shut things out.

"Obviously, I'm a firm believer now."

As for the "other side," Jenny Ellen learned early on that she could have conscious contact with other realms of consciousness.

Messages from Other Realms

In keeping with having a secret life, in early years Jenny Ellen was silent about communication she sometimes received from other dimensions. For many years the contact was sporadic, at least on a conscious level.

"I guess the first time I heard a voice outside of my head, very clearly, was telling me that I was going to marry a certain person. I had only met the person briefly ... I remember thinking, well, if I'm supposed to, okay. And I remember thinking, too, I thought he was engaged, but I guess if he's supposed to marry me, he'll get unengaged. I remember not feeling any great emotion at all. It was just, this was what was supposed to be.

"But you see," Jenny explained, "when you get messages from higher levels, they don't carry emotions with them. You can get into emotions afterward. But when it's a stronger message of destiny, it *comes* from a higher level that has a sense of knowing with it, but not emotion. And then, as you bring that knowing down in, then you can add your emotion to it."

That man *did* get unengaged, and they did marry. For the first fifteen years of the marriage, he was not aware that Jenny Ellen had unusual abilities and abiding interests.

"When it came out years later, it really, really upset him. A mutual friend explained [to him] that this was not that bad, that kind of thing. I think he [her husband] said, 'They used to burn people at the stake for this.'

"I would just use it in what I was working with. Like, one time I got up and had the feeling I needed to clean house and go to the store ... and I got back, and my in-laws called, and they were in town and wanted to come over. House was clean. Lunch was fixed. Cookies baked. So it was just daily living things.

"But you see, I was so used to living that part of my life very separate. I learned that as a child, that that part of my life was very, shall we say, secretive, very personal. And that was nothing to live that way. In fact, it was strange to talk about it … and I still prefer not to talk about this with most people … It's not that it's not part of my everyday life, it's just not part of the everyday discussion."

Jenny Ellen recalled another time when such a voice first spoke to her. "There was a time I was in the kitchen—this was years later—and there was this voice that said, 'You won't be in this house next year.' And it was like, 'Oh, okay.' And many times when I got those messages like that, I didn't have any question about them … It would be, like, okay if that's supposed to happen, it'll just happen on its own; I don't have to get caught up in it. It was nice not to have to be caught up in it.

"You see, at first that kind of thing would happen just spontaneously, and then later, I developed where I could ask questions and get the answers back. It would be different from going into deep prayer and asking."

Conscious Communication with Spiritual Realms

Jenny Ellen eventually asked for conscious communication with her guides on the other side, to be able to ask questions of them and to get answers. It came. And it nearly drove her to distraction. She would have an idle thought, such as, "I wonder about this or that," and the answer would come right away, and in more detail and volume than she expected or wanted. They answered her *every* inquiry. She might be thinking rather idly to herself, "I wonder if the mailman's coming." And she would hear back the likes of, "Yes, he's coming. He's stopped to talk to so-and-so. He's four houses down. He'll be here in about …"

Her voice escalates at the memory of it.

"And it was like, good gravy! I didn't mean for somebody to answer every little thought I had. I finally yelled, 'Take it away!' And it went. And then I was like, now what have I done? So then I asked for it to come back, not steady, but once in a while, and not so loud."

She said, instead of it being outside of her head, the communication gradually came to where it was inside. But again, it was like hitting a sounding board.

"You can tell by the vibration that it's them and not my thoughts. And sometimes, when they've dictated things to me, I put my own interpretation in, and they said, 'Now wait a minute, that's not what we said.'"

Meditation and the Other Side

When Jenny Ellen first allowed herself to seriously explore metaphysical possibilities, there weren't many books available, so she mostly consulted her Bible and her clairaudient guidance, until more material came out in the sixties. She developed a rich inner life and stunningly clear contact with her guides from the spiritual realms.

"I didn't have guidance from books, and in some ways I missed that," she said. "When I found out what was there [later], I thought, 'Oh my, how I could have developed.' But in other ways—the trouble if you do a lot of reading without experiencing, you know *about*. But I was forced to learn more through the *experience*, than through somebody else's experience.

"I could go into meditation for a couple of hours and just be told all sorts of things about other dimensions and other ways of being, so I was taught that way. So when I did get books, a lot of it was just confirmation of what I'd already been taught. Which was good, I mean, it was nice to see that confirmation. Sometimes you begin to wonder how daft you are. But the other thing is, that built a trust level: the fact that they would tell me things and, then later, I would read it in a book."

Jenny said her relationship with her guides evolved and developed over time. She once asked them, if they were so high up (spiritually), why they fooled with such small things with her, and they said they were developing a trust base.

"I had a lot of direct voice contact on just everyday living ... and, then again, that built a trust level. That's one of the biggest things: that you have to have a trust level with the guides and angels that you work with. You have to be able to recognize their vibrations; otherwise, it's like lower-level entities or somebody who has just passed over [through death] can be telling you anything. You have to learn to sense what's a higher vibration, and what isn't."

Jenny distinguishes between angels and guides or, at least, *her* guides. She said, as she understands it, angels are a different form from people and work directly with God. She believes her guides to be beings who once lived on earth, who are highly evolved, and who don't have to incarnate anymore, unless they choose to. Generally, they seek to assist from one of the levels of the spirit world. She believes her guides are high-level beings who do God's work and God's will from one of the higher levels of consciousness.

As to whether or not she's ever had any source try to influence her that was *not* on such a lofty level as her own good guides, Jenny said yes.

"But I knew right away that it wasn't them, that it was … a person who had died and basically wanted a lot of attention," she said. "I did talk to the guides about it [later], and they said that many people who have died and are in the lower astral plane want attention. They don't necessarily want things any better, they just want attention, and it's best not to get involved with them.

"Then," she added, "there are people who've passed on to the other side that want to visit sometimes. If it's somebody I knew, I might visit some, but I'm not into spending a lot of time talking with them."

Her First Reading

Years ago, people did not often speak of having conscious communication with other dimensions. Still, some people eventually became aware that Jenny Ellen did have special abilities, and she received her first request for an intuitive reading. By this time, her husband had accepted and even embraced her interest in metaphysics, and they had moved to the States from Canada. Jenny recalled her first reading, how it came about, and why she thought she could do it.

"She [the client] was so insistent that she wanted one, and it was like, 'Oh, we'll just see what's there.' She was happy with it. She sent her friends. If she hadn't, my life would've been different. And then, the other thing was that somebody else had recommended me and said that I could do it."

Jenny said during the reading she saw pictures in her mind's eye and sometimes literally saw them. In order to find the answers to her client's questions, she searched for them. She explained somewhat how that process worked.

"I just sat there, and whatever came to me I told her. I assume she had some questions … I one'd myself into the heart area, and the answer might be there. It might show up in my head. I might see pictures. It can come in feelings … and then I have to sit and sort it out."

Ironically, or according to what Jenny Ellen laughingly calls God's choreography, her husband eventually began a relationship with the very woman who was Jenny's first client. Jenny's marriage to him soon ended.

Jenny Ellen had actually been forewarned by her guides that she and her husband would not always be together. She asked if they could stay together until the children were out of school and heard, "Your wish is granted."

With her previous life in tatters and her new one a fledgling endeavor, Jenny Ellen moved away from her ex-husband and the home they shared and started over, in a sweet rural state far from the madding crowd and, as always, with God at her side.

Giving Readings to Family Members and Other Intuitives

Jenny Ellen lives a rather quiet, yet full life. She has hobbies. She grows roses that the deer sometimes nibble. She has an especially beloved pet. She travels for workshops. She writes books. Many students are also clients, and her phone rings frequently. She produces new material for her classes. She's involved with a local church. Her children and grandchildren call and visit. Sometimes, she gives readings to family members.

"One of the funniest ones was [when] I asked my daughter something about her mother. My eyes were closed while I was checking in [during the reading], and I was so into what was going on." She laughs merrily at the remembrance of it. "That's an interesting feeling, doing a reading on [grown] children and seeing how the aspect of mother affects them. And it's, 'Whoops, do I want to tell this?'" And she laughs heartily yet again.

Rarely, but occasionally, she gets a reading herself and sometimes quite successfully so.

"Sometimes when I've had a reading, I can feel the reader's energy solidly connected with mine. It's like we're right together. I feel a truth level; it really resonates.

"Now, sometimes I haven't fully agreed with what they've said, but I then, on my own … take that information later and say what did this mean, what else. It just needed to be shaded a little bit differently or just a little different interpretation."

Jenny enjoys giving readings for other psychics and intuitives.

"It's fun to do readings on people who read, because they understand," she said.

She said, though she may tire sometimes physically, she doesn't get tired of doing readings. They still hold interest for her.

"It's always of interest to me because *I* don't know what's going to be there, and *I* learn a lot," she said.

Meditation as a Means to More

Meditation is a major subject for Jenny Ellen. She is a master of various forms of meditation, has written books on it, teaches it, and uses it to obtain guidance and information.

"To me, meditation is a listening, a tuning in and listening. [Some] people like to blank their minds and that's one form, where they totally try to keep any thoughts out. If a person isn't very developed and they're doing that, there's a real tendency for some lower-level entities to come in, if they [the meditators] don't raise their vibrations first. I much prefer being open to the energies, stilling my own thoughts; it's like stilling my brain.

"Our brain is like a computer and it works with what's been put in there, what's been programmed into it, and it can just run run run over the same things all the time; but if we can *still* that, let the brain be still, then higher mind comes in, because we all have access to cosmic mind, mind of God. And then, when we're still, ideas and information, all sorts of things, can come from [higher] mind."

According to Jenny Ellen, when you're on a higher vibration, lower-level entities can't reach you to communicate, and they soon lose interest.

"It's a waste of their time," she said, "You're no fun."

Before Each Reading

Jenny Ellen goes into prayer before each reading and asks if there is anything she needs to know before the session. She asks if there is anything she needs to tell the client.

"That helps put me in tune with the person," she said. "And then, I try to live in a prayer state. So I don't feel that I always have to go into a long prayer about this or that. Because it feels that I'm there."

Jenny Ellen doesn't ask for protection before a reading because prayer is a natural protection that elevates her to a higher level. She works from the heart, which forms a natural protection. In fact, in order to read for a person, Jenny has to open her heart and to really love that person.

"If I don't open my heart chakra, I can't work well with the person," Jenny explained.

When she speaks of love, it is not a sentimental conjured love, rather it is a universal love energy, brought forth by an act of will. This works best for Jenny, although she acknowledged that it might be otherwise for other psychics and intuitives.

"I put my consciousness in that area [heart] … So you find out where your energy works best in your body. If you work a good deal through your subconscious, you may want that [open] as well as the heart. And having the upper back open at the same time that you open the heart gives more strength … wherever you're open in your body. You will still process things through your head, because that's important too, but you can't just do things through the head, because you lose too much."

Jenny mentioned another protection for her: When the client leaves, she simply lets their energies leave with them.

On rare occasions, she gets a sense that she isn't supposed to read for someone. In those instances, she generally refers them to someone else, such as a therapist or another intuitive.

Where Answers Are Found During a Session

Jenny considered where an answer may be found when someone asks a question during an intuitive session. She said often it comes into the heart and the head at the same time.

"And it's like, as I'm talking, I see the words or feel the words just before I say them. But it can be different at different times."

Jenny has a level of regard for some of the information she conveys.

"I am very surprised sometimes by some answers that come out," she said.

Sometimes she feels a need to go deeper into her intuitive level. She does this by opening her heart and thinking about the situation or the question being asked.

"[I then ask] is there something else [I] need to know about it?" Jenny said. Sometimes, she feels called to pray for a person or to advise the client to pray for someone in his or her life.

"The interesting thing is, you have to have no attachment to the outcome. You have to leave it in God's hands. Because many times, when things are calls to prayer, you don't know what comes. And you have to know that you are the channel, one could say, for the prayer to go through; but you have to be selfless enough that you're not attached to what God does with it.

"It's like God *wants* us to ask for things for other people. When we ask for things for ourselves and other people, we open the channels to receive them. It's like God has these gifts for us, but if we don't open to receive, we pretty much got to get hit on the head to get them. It's like, many times, our prayers, our asking something, are prayers that God has put in our hearts to ask for."

The Intuitive as Mystic, and Dark Night of the Soul

For Jenny Ellen, the mystical path has been part of the journey.

"Mysticism deals with the inner self as well as the outer self," she said. "And if you're going to be a good intuitive, you need to develop that area … And of course, the mystical has to do with the mysteries, things hidden."

Jenny Ellen used to have depression, and she eventually discovered value in those low periods.

"I can't stay in any state long without wanting to know why am I here? What's the good side [for she believes there is a positive side to everything]? So I started to explore that. And it's like, depression opens you to a deep inner self, and so I got a lot of mileage from that, once I really dealt with that and opened up … I'll [still] be pulled into the inner life, what you'll call the inner world, but it doesn't feel depressing."

Jenny Ellen now values those periods of depression.

"I would've missed so much of inner wisdom, inner strength. The reason it feels depressing is because the energy is so heavy, and you feel like you fell into a well. But if you say, 'Oh, I'm in the well. Let's see, does this one have sides to it? What can I see here?' If you accept the fact that you're there and work with it, I think that makes the difference. And I think anybody who goes through spiritual growth goes through the dark night of the soul, and I certainly went through that."

The dark night of the soul descended upon her and stayed for weeks upon weeks, she said. And though it was difficult, she felt it was purposeful.

"The dark night of the soul is so that you open very deeply within, and you gain such inner strength and inner wisdom and you gain a deep knowing," Jenny said. "You're just not rattled around like you can be otherwise … you clean out deeply, so that you open up deeply. Because you can't go higher into the spiritual world if you haven't gone deeper into one's inner self. That's part of your spiritual growth. It opens to the mystical side."

Jenny said one aspect of the dark night could be a sense that God cannot be reached. Others may turn away from you, or seem to. You need faith to sustain yourself, she said.

"Although I felt like I couldn't reach God and that, I *knew* I still could; I still had the faith. I *knew* this was something I needed to go through. I didn't understand all of it at the time; I learned more about the mechanics of it later. If you don't have that faith, it's pretty hard."

The Nature of Her Guides

The story of Jenny Ellen's relationship with her guides is remarkable. Although they have been in contact for decades, and there are many touching stories about their relationship, Jenny spent many years in relative silence about them and their role in her life. In earlier years, she was aware of working specifically with two guides named in esoteric literature as Ascended Masters of the Great White Brotherhood (white is a reference to light not race, as race is not a factor). However, her guides change, she said, though some go out and come back into communication with her later. Her guides prefer not to be known by names or to be associated with nationalities.

"They say, 'Why would I want to [know]?' That they would have been many nationalities; they would have been many names," Jenny said. "Any time, if I would have put a name or a nationality, it limits. When they're higher-level guides, and they work with higher things, it's like they're working with the God force, and it doesn't matter [what name or nationality]; it's like I recognize them from their vibrations. Because we all have soul vibrations.

"There are some persons [in this work] who just do better with names," Jenny said. "Somebody explained it to me this way: A person who is into the more abstract thinking will relate to God better, but a person who has to have a more concrete form will relate to Jesus better, or whatever spiritual personage. And it's the same, if you can have a more abstract approach to this, then you don't have to label them with names or whatever; you don't have to pigeonhole them. And then, it opens more what you can get from them. But some people are built so that they need the other and then that's different. Now, I'm not saying that because they have names that they're lower-level ones, but, usually, the higher-level ones don't want to get into that."

The Ascended Masters are thought to be the guardians of humanity. This group has been known in some esoteric circles for centuries, and they are said to hail from the upper vibratory levels of the spirit world.

Once, Jenny Ellen's relationship with her guides was such that they asked her to pray for people who needed it—people Jenny did not know. She said one time at an event, a woman came forth and was introduced to the crowd. Jenny recognized her name as one of the people she had been asked to pray for. Jenny said it wasn't that her guides asked her to pray that the woman be healed, but rather that she be better able to handle her illness.

Jenny recalled many such stories of this remarkable relationship with her guides. The range of their communication has varied, from something as small as their directing her on where to find a good deal on a piece of furniture to loftier matters. Jenny Ellen, however, doesn't believe she's had the same guides all her life, but certain ones return.

"My understanding is you have a guardian angel that stays with you through all of your life. And then you have different angels and guides, depending on what you're doing ... what you're working on, what your projects are.

"It feels like some are there for a while and then move out and then come back later. There's one [guide] that seems to be more of a taskmaster and a little bossy, and that one moves in and out. Once when I was driving near the [Chicago airport], I said I was lost and needed some help and he said—it feels like a he—'You are *not* lost. You know *exactly* where you are.' And I did. I was at the corner of such and such, in such and such a suburb. He said, 'What you want to know is how to get from there to the airport.' I said, 'Well, yeah.' He said, 'Then ask that.'

"Sometimes, if I'm doing a session too long, he'll say, 'That's enough. You wind it up.' And if I don't, it's like my head is erased. There's just no way [to continue], and then I say, 'I have to quit.' And [the client] says, 'But but.' It's usually past the time anyway, and it's like I can't help it."

Jenny does not consider the question of whether these guides from other realms might ever appear on earth to be a topic of great interest. They are already here, she said, in a manner of speaking.

"How would that be different from them being consciously among humanity now?" she asked.

Astrology and Evolution as Cooperative Partners

Jenny actually discovered that we carry our astrology charts in the energy fields around our bodies. She reads this during sessions with clients. She does not know of anyone who uses this technique.

Jenny considers whether or not she believes that she had a part in constructing *her* astrology chart prior to this life.

"Yes, probably," she accedes.

However, she doesn't think that we all help to plan our charts; she believes it depends on our degree of evolvement—an area she sees as too often overlooked.

"My understanding is, the more evolved you are, the more you have choice; and the lesser evolved persons or the ones not that interested in their growth would kind of wait until karma kind of pulled them in. Because certain energies can set up a resonance that would attract the karma that someone has.

"Evolution is not looked at enough," she said firmly. She believes that earth is the planet of evolution. And she believes that every possibility has an alternative side.

"I do not believe that anything's negative just to be negative," she said.

Jenny Ellen believes for every negative there is a positive. By way of example, she said the positive side of envy is aspiration.

When She Is Not to Know, and Things Unexpected

Jenny said there are times in a reading when she feels that she is not to know something.

"Oh yes, oh yes," she said. "Well, first of all I'm kind of aware that there's just a blankness there. Or sometimes the words will come, 'They're not supposed to know, and we're not going to let you know either because you might tell ...'

"Many times they'll [guides] tell me, 'No, later on, you can ask that question but not right now.' And I'm glad when they don't tell me if I'm not supposed to tell, because then I don't have to think about it.

"And then there are times when I'm doing a session that I get told something and told, 'This is for your information; the person shouldn't even know something was said about it.' So that becomes for *my* growth, as I'm watching what's happening with the person.

"Sometimes, if I'm picking up on something [but haven't gotten it yet], I can get really heavy or disconnected. Then I know I've missed something, that there's more to that, there's more to the answer, and then I go back [deeper] and say, 'Okay' [what?]."

As with most high-level intuitives, Jenny said often clients contact her for assistance with one matter only to find that there was something greater that they need to consider.

"Sometimes people will come in with one question; they think that's the burning question, only to find that, no, that caught their attention, but there was something bigger that was going on that they hadn't addressed yet."

When doing a reading for someone, every good intuitive should be aware of the energies asking to be considered, she said, even if the client has not indicated those as areas of interest.

"In doing the session, one needs to be aware of those energies that are just calling to be checked," she said.

It is sometimes helpful in an intuitive reading if the client allows the intuitive to address what comes up, rather than trying to direct them to only specific concerns, she said.

What She Sees But Doesn't Share

Generally, Jenny does not tell a client when she sees death or divorce. She believes that doing so may interfere with the person's growth or free will. Furthermore, there are other ways of helping the person, without disclosing such momentous events prematurely. She feels strongly about not disclosing death.

"Some others may disagree and may feel that it's all right for them to do it," she said, "but it doesn't feel all right for me to talk about when somebody's going to die, because we have some say over our death … [plus] if there's someone who thinks there's someone who's going to die, it changes how they relate to that person, and it just totally shifts the energy. And what if you're wrong? I just feel [that] what it does to a person is very hard. Now, when somebody asks about it, I do like to address the situation of really living their life with that person, really enjoying them, really visiting with them, not ending up saying, 'I wish I would've said this; I wish I would've asked that' … You don't have to regret the leftover energy that wasn't expressed."

Unless there are strong reasons for doing so, Jenny prefers not to predict divorce and instead seeks to address problems in the marriage or discuss work the person needs to do on himself or herself.

"Sometimes people will ask, are they going to divorce this person or not, and sometimes it's so strong that it needs to be said, but most of the time I won't, because it takes away their free will, as to whether they decide what they're going to do," Jenny said. "What I choose to do is address what's going on [in the relationship], and in some cases I have told them, 'It doesn't matter if you divorce or if you don't divorce; what matters now is you've got to build up your own strength and build up your own life ... Don't be making any decisions based on weakness. Get your strength back. And [then], see who you are.'"

Jenny believes predicting divorce may cause people to give up too soon and thereby lose opportunities for growth and development.

"Let's say somebody goes to a psychic and they're told, 'You're going to divorce this person in six months.' How's that person going to react for the next six months? You're going to totally distance yourself from the spouse. You're going to be angry with the spouse. What learnings are lost!

"With any marriage, I think they should really try and work things out, because if they give up too soon, like if somebody says, 'Oh you're going to get divorced,' and then they just give up and then three or four months later they're divorced and they haven't *tried* to develop more of a connection, more of a relationship, they've missed some growth. So it's like, build up your strength, and then you'll know better what to do.

"And then I'll tell them, '*If* you divorce, you need to look look look at this. If you don't divorce, you need to look look look at this.' Because we always have these probable futures."

When Giving Answers May Interfere with a Client's Growth

Sometimes Jenny sees something in a session but gets the impression or is told that the client is not to know about it. She expounded on this.

"You never, in doing a session, should knowingly take away a person's growth because, if you take away their growth in something, they're going to have to go back and do it again. And it could be more difficult the next time. But discussing probabilities, options, things are there that could be done, new ways of looking at things, [is] invaluable help."

Sometimes clients just want her to give them answers. Often, their learning could be more important than "knowing."

"There'll be times when I'm doing a session on somebody and I'm given the answer but told not to tell the person, because it would interfere with their growth, because sometimes you have to go through a certain amount of growth before you get an answer. And if they get the answer ahead of time and don't do the work, then it doesn't fit, and it doesn't click [with them]. But if they go through the pattern themselves ...

"Now, I can give them some guidance on that, ways to work with it, and they go through that, then they own it, they know it's theirs, they can feel it, they can do it. And that's the important thing. You don't ever, ever want to take away anybody's growth with this. So I don't try to say it has to be this way or that way, 'It's like, if you want it to work out this way, then you do la-di-dah-di-dah'—you know? Because we do have a number of probable futures. At all times.

"There are some things that are so strongly destined that they're pretty much going to happen regardless of what a person does, but what you do in preparing for them or opening to them can make all the difference in how you handle them."

Different Needs in Marriages, and Loneliness

Jenny Ellen returned to the subject of marriage, as if it were a matter that asked to be addressed. She said there are many different types of marriages that meet different people's needs. People can be misguided in trying to maneuver their marriage into something they *think* they should have, which, in actuality, may not work well for them.

"There are a number of marriages that are, really, almost business arrangements, and seem to be what the persons need," she said. "Each marriage is different. Sometimes, when they're not all lovey dovey, each person develops more of themselves and goes on to *be* more of themselves. It's like they have this union, they have the connection, they have the partner, but they also are living their own destiny energy stronger.

"And then you'll find some that are just very connected and that seems fine, but that's a different energy pattern and it's like, what suits each person, each relationship ... You have to look at what you want out of a marriage, what fulfills your needs, and forget these so-called ideals."

Jenny believes that we can expect too much of a partner, especially if our relationship with God is underdeveloped, and it can lead to a sense of loneliness.

"I think when you're more open to other dimensions, there's not that loneliness," she said. "And I think, basically, loneliness is loneliness for God anyway. And I believe that all roads lead to God, but some people that are so lonely for this person or that are basically lonely for God. If a person loves God first, then all relationships are going to be better, because you don't attach that much to a relationship. When the other person has to take the place of God for you, that's too big a burden on that other person. And you're going to be disappointed. There's no way that they can ever fulfill that. No one person can become everything to someone else. They might be that or seem that for a little while, but it fades away. It becomes too much of a burden on the other person. And so—and this is one of the things I like to tell people [in sessions]—'Get your relationship with God together first, then your relationship with others will be better and in better proportion.'"

Even though her contact with other dimensions is rich, she has known loneliness.

"Speaking of the loneliness though, if I'm around people too intensely for too long, then I'm lonely for the deeper connection with God, and I'll have to stop right in the middle of being with people and tune back into that connection, or just keep that connection going all the time around those people. But you can't always get as deep as you'd like to when you're around other people. So sometimes there's that need to pull away and do that."

Past Life Readings and Regressions

Jenny has been doing past life readings and regressions for so long that she doesn't quite remember when she started. When a person's previous lives appear to her, it is as if she is watching a movie. While watching it, she gets the *thoughts* and the *feelings* that the person was having at the time. She doesn't always reach for a past life consciously during a session.

"Sometimes I'll be seeing something and ... alongside it I see the energy of a past life that's affecting it, and I like to tell those to the person then, because you get a better understanding, if you know that the cause was another life, and this is what's manifesting with it," Jenny said.

Again, she is cautious about what she shares with the client.

"There are some times I'll sense past lives, and I'll tell the person, 'I'd rather just tell you a few things. I don't want you to re-experience it; it's too heavy for now ...' I'll tell them whatever they can know to learn from, but you don't want to tell them about something that's so traumatic that it messes them up in this life as well."

Sometimes it can be interesting to see our past lives, but, ultimately, she said, we should have higher intentions for searching into lives once lived.

"Past lives should be to help in one's growth," she said.

If a seemingly negative life appears, it might be beneficial to the client for Jenny to look first and see why they were involved in that, what they were learning, before disclosing it to the client. She said then, if she tells them about it, it's easier for the person to handle, because she has put it in a meaningful context. She would not necessarily regress them (take them back to it).

"There's no reason for them to have to re-experience it," she said simply.

On the other hand, Jenny may tell a client of a past life and invite them to experience a certain part of it, if it seems beneficial.

"There are times when I might be doing a reading and see a past life, and I stop and have them experience it, just because it's some feeling they need to have in their body now. Let's say for instance, they had a much stronger body [then], and they need to *feel* what it's like to have a strong body now, to help them get that in this life. That would be a reason."

While Jenny Ellen does not see value in regressing a person to experience a past life trauma, if the person was to get there on their own, she would help guide them.

"Let's say that a person was in a past life [regression] and all of a sudden [they were] aware of being raped or some such thing. I wouldn't purposefully take them there, but if they just got there, then I would ask them, 'Where are you feeling the greatest pain in your body?' Many times rape victims feel a loss of power. 'Did you feel a loss of power? If you did, where did you feel it in your body? And what are you carrying in your body from that life to this life that holds you back?' And then, [I advise them] to forgive the other person, themselves, the situation, and to ask that it all be blessed and turn to good.

"I don't ever leave anybody with something bad without them working with it. Where does it affect the body? How does it affect the body? How does it affect the life?"

If something bad was done to a person in a previous life, often they did that same thing to someone else in another life, although this is not always the case.

"We need to teach people that those are not good ways of expressing oneself. Let's say a rapist had been raped by a person in a previous life; that's what I call Old Testament karma because it does talk about an eye for an eye and a tooth for a tooth. A lot in New Testament [however] is forgiveness and understanding and not having to suffer the consequences, because you understand and achieve forgiveness and, it's like, what can you learn, what can you do better? Otherwise it's the same old stuff over and over and over and over."

Why Good Intuitives May Be Wrong

Jenny Ellen believes good intuitives can be wrong in their predictions, for a number of reasons.

"It could very definitely be that the person [client] has chosen a different probable future, that's one thing," she said. "Another thing is, the person, let's say something good is supposed to come through, [but] the person is so negative that it can't manifest through them. Also, a person has certain things they have to do before certain things will manifest. You've got to open the letter to read it, you know.

"And then, hey, it's easy to be wrong sometimes because, if you get a picture or a message, sometimes it looks like it would interpret this way, but it really interprets another. And that just happens sometimes."

Jenny Ellen believes that everything that a good psychic gets is correct, but that it is in the interpretation where they often err. She sometimes asks her guides what a symbol is meant to convey, or she takes it into her body to see what she *feels* for the interpretation.

"Another thing to watch for is when you see something sometime, is that symbolic? Or is it literal? I feel it in my body ... Symbols will come from the feeling level, and you have to go back to the feeling level to interpret them ... to go back to the feeling level, you feel it in your body."

Also, the client may simply choose not to make the effort to achieve something that was seen as possible.

"There are other things that one can see that are possibilities, but the person may flat out not want to make the exertion to go through with them, because we all have a number of possibilities that we don't have to follow through on. We can take that possibility and make something happen with it [or not]."

Vintage Insights on Giving Readings

Things That Surprise Her

One of the things that most surprises Jenny Ellen in her readings is how much people limit themselves.

"People don't take their potential seriously enough," she said. "It takes a first step and then a second step and God *will* act through us, but we have to take the steps. God can give us the energy and the direction, the motivation, all sorts of things, but we're the ones that have to take the steps. We're the arms and legs and mouths and so on that can go ahead and do it.

"I'm just thrilled when people glimpse something about themselves and then take hold and do it ... It's lack of vision for most people."

The way the energies and evolution are going now, she said, people should not think that just because once they didn't have talent or ability in a certain area, they still don't. Greater potential is there with the new energies that have arrived.

"The energies are so busy now that people are finding that they have a lot of talents and abilities that they've never had before or that they can learn quicker, that it's happening quicker," she said.

Seeking Guidance for the Self

In seeking self-guidance, Jenny Ellen believes that often the body knows what we may not.

"I open up inside the body and ask the question from there," she said. "And then just sit and allow an answer to form. It takes a little longer sometimes when you're doing it for yourself because you're more emotionally involved in it. And you have to get past that. But one of the things that stops a lot of people from developing this is they're not quiet and let the answer form. The answer has to literally form before you can get it. Now, sometimes, they form quickly, and sometimes they take a longer time. Using the prayer state is a good way to do that. If you pray for an answer—if you're in prayer when you ask for an answer—then you've got to be still and listen."

Finding a consensus among the aspects of ourselves is helpful, Jenny said. By focusing on the solar plexus, a person may tune into what's already in process, what's already manifesting. Then, you can take your question into both the heart and the solar plexus and see if it resonates. If you get an *ugh*, then it does not fit. But if it feels good in both areas, that's an indication of the affirmative. The body, some say, knows truth.

"It needs to resonate with the heart … but also with the head. It needs to resonate with the whole body. The heart may need something else … and we end up confused. But if the head feels good about it and the heart—if it feels good in the body—your body's going to know things that your head doesn't."

Jenny acknowledges that conducting the universe of ourselves can sometimes be confusing, but it's an orchestration she has long loved and sought to conduct with proficiency.

Doing Readings from a Distance

Since energy easily transcends distances, Jenny Ellen does do readings by phone, but she prefers to first do a reading for the client in person, because then she's better aware of their energy pattern.

However, there have been exceptions. She once did a reading for a client who called her from another country, whom she had never met. She remembers that consultation with a smile.

"I had a guy in Australia over the phone and I said, 'The back of your head's too tight. That skin's too tight.' He said, 'Well, I'm so vain. I had strips cut out and put in the front.'"

The client had had a hair transplant and Jenny Ellen, with her acute ability to go where the energy takes her, picked up on it.

"I had him after that," she said, laughing.

She thinks the phone works well enough, although she didn't always do sessions by phone. She believes phones themselves are better now, but she has a problem with cell phones.

"I don't like to do [readings] over cell phones," Jenny said, "The energy of the phone is so strong, it's hard to pick up on the person. I have to weed through that."

Discerning the Origin of a Thought-form

Jenny advises working intuitives to be careful to distinguish whether something they pick up on in a person's energy field is the client's, or if what they're sensing was put there by someone else.

"One thing to watch out for in doing sessions ... is, for instance, there may be in the person's energy field a thought-form to go into a certain [career] field. But if you look closely, that [may be] a thought-form put there by a parent or someone else close to them. And that person will feel that thought-form and kind of think they should [do it], but since they haven't fully owned it or invested in it, then it hangs as a thought-form.

"Now, with some people, it can be so strong that they'll take that thought-form as though it's their own and then find it very difficult to do that [career], and then sometime they wake up and say, 'Hey! I never wanted to do this! It was this person or that person that wanted me to do that. I really want to do thus-and-so.'

"And then, what they do, when they have that moment of truth with their *own* energy, that clarity—it's like it shatters the thought-form that the other person placed on them. The force of their own clarity [shatters it]."

Finding the Flip Side of a Negative

If something negative is in a person's chart, so, then, is something positive.

"I always look for the positive side of something. So, when I see the negative, I see the positive right away with it," she said. "They are opposite sides of the same coin. If you take care of the positive, the negative doesn't have to happen.

"One thing that can come through in a session is finding better ways they can use their free will … We can choose to work through positive things or negative. I prefer the positive. It will stay until we work with it or it turns negative and we say, 'Okay, okay, what do I need to do here …'

"*Learn* to use the energies. It's like saying, what's my best choice. Let it pass through me gently."

As for psychics who stir up fear in their clients, Jenny has an opinion about their motivation.

"If you put more fear in things, you get more control … It may be their way of trying to get you to come back, if they're feeding you fearful things. Bringing fear into other people is, many times, a need for control. I've had people [come in] and say, 'Can you fix it? Reinterpret what they saw and said.'"

Any pattern we carry has a positive side, she said, even genetic tendencies that at first appear problematic.

Jenny said counseling people to understand genetic tendencies and find positive ways of working with them has the dual effect of helping the offspring to understand themselves *and* their parents and to have empathy for their parents.

"They understand then what goes on with the parent more and then there's sympathy for the parent that they couldn't handle [the energies], and not a rejection of the parent … So helping people to understand genetic energies and how they influence things, I think, is an important part of this kind of work."

Turning Trials into Blessings

Jenny believes we can be transformers and change the negative to the positive, with sustained effort perhaps. Clearly, she believes that understanding energy patterns and astrological arrangements can help people find positive ways of using the energies available to them.

"I've seen times when persons are really good workers, but they get fired, and many times it's because they are *such* good workers that they take over and act like it's their company, and they forget that they're hired. In some cases ... I say, 'Look, you have so much leadership energy ... in your energy pattern, that you will scare a boss into thinking that you want their job'—and sometimes they do—'But maybe you need to take your leadership and start your own business.' And persons who have done that have turned out to be very successful, but [others] haven't realized that the very energy that got them fired from other places could make them do well in their own business. They just feel like a failure."

A good intuitive can give constructive insights.

"When you use the intuitive, it brings in other things that don't show and will bring in more of a reason of what you're supposed to be getting with it, and maybe alternative ways of doing it."

Destinies, Great and Small

"The more you get into this, the more you set your foot on the [spiritual] path, the more you've got to follow that destiny stuff," Jenny said. "But you can't say to somebody, 'I maybe can't go on that trip because destiny might tell me something else.'"

She laughs. "And there've been times where there would be an organizational meeting or something that I should go to, but I'll sense right away that, no, there's something else. And I just have to say, 'No, that day is taken.' Even though there's nothing on the calendar. And I don't know what it is. Then by the time that day comes, I find out what it is. So you just plain can't tell everybody everything.

"Some people understand the destiny stuff very well and others think you're being a little high flown, thinking about destiny. But little things can be destined as well as big things. A lot of people have asked [in readings] what their destiny or purpose was. And that's so difficult to answer because, it might be their destiny to go to the neighbors and help them out with some problem, as well as it might be a destiny to write a book or give a speech. We all have a number of destinies. We all have a number of purposes. I think one of the things is, people want one big destiny or purpose, so they can hurry up and do that and then sit around free. And that's not how life goes.

"Here's something else that came out the other day: If a person does a lot of good, if you're always doing good works, but you don't do them from love, they have a tendency to turn negative. It becomes busy work, or the person may not want that particular good for themselves, like that old lady being helped by the Boy Scout [story about forcing help on the little old lady]. So when you do good things, it better be from the heart."

The Importance of the Aura

Although Jenny Ellen can see the energy fields around people (called an aura), she prefers to sense them. She can get more information if she doesn't have to deal with the issues of interpreting colors and shadings.

"Some persons' colors are very flat and dull and other persons' are very radiant," Jenny said. "Of course, the radiant, light ones are a much higher level, much higher development."

She believes our auras are a protective sheath and that we should use them as such. She also believes that we are far more sensitive to one another than we might imagine.

"If your own aura is strong enough, you're not going to be picking up other people's things all the time. And if your aura is weak, you can pick up other people's physical things, their emotional and mental things ... and so, the strengthening of the aura is the best thing to do, because then, that's there all the time. You don't have to say, 'Oh, do I need to be shutting something out?'"

With a strong aura, you can afford to be sensitive.

"The other thing is, when you've strengthened your aura, you still feel the stuff on the outside edge, and you know that this person is upset, or that person is negative toward you that day, or whatever. You still know those things, but you *know* that it's someone else's, it doesn't come in and you own it and think that it's yours. That's the big thing is knowing what's *your* feeling, what's *your* illness, what's *your* stuff.

You just don't want to be picking up [other people's stuff], especially if you're going to be in the intuitive field. You need to be able to pick things up, and if you're forever shutting off, then that limits what you can pick up."

Jenny has identified certain activities that strengthen the aura.

"Physical exercise helps to strengthen the aura," she said. "Walking helps to strengthen the aura. Anything that gets your energy from inside of you, out around you, strengthens the aura. Meditating with colors and feeling them in you and around you. If you focus on your own center—you can do solar plexus or heart—and take deep peaceful breaths … Your aura is caused by your energy."

Too often people fail to appreciate the aura's significance. "People don't understand the importance of the aura," Jenny said. "Like I said, it can color what you send out in the moment. Your thoughts can be so pure, but if you've got muddiness in your aura, that'll give you problems. As well, somebody else's positive energies coming around can be muddied by what's in your aura.

"Following along on that same line, if you listen to a lot of scary things, scary movies, things that rattle your aura, rattle your body, you're putting negative stuff in the aura. You're messing up your auric pattern."

Higher Vibrations Attract Higher Levels and Vice Versa

Jenny advises raising our vibrations before we meditate, do intuitive work, or reach for any inspired contact. Otherwise, we may court the undesirable.

"If you're going to work with intuition, you're already on a higher level because that's a more spiritual level, but a lot of psychic things do come from the emotional level," she said. "But if you raise your vibrations so that you're coming more from the intuitive level, then those things [making contact with lower-level entities] aren't so liable to happen. You may hear a lower-level entity, but you would know. Your intuitions would tell you … be careful. Whereas, if you're just into the astral level, well, you can get caught up emotionally with the negative ones. And the negative ones *love* to get a hold of a person on the emotional level, because then they've got them. And usually they'll promise things like true love or money or wonderful things happening.

"They'll promise that kind of thing to keep the person connected."

Higher-level guides are not inclined to promise a lot of things. She said they are more interested in guiding the person in what they're doing at the moment, in teaching them, or in bringing in information, and they will not say that the person will become rich or the like.

Some people have lower-level connections, and they don't mind, but they should, she said.

"I've known some very intelligent people who have had lower-level connections, and although nothing they [their connections] said ever came true, they still wanted the connection, just because they liked to hear the voice, they liked that connection of talking to someone," Jenny said. "And it's not healthy in the long run. The excitement of connecting with the other side, that needs to be tempered by who you're talking with.

"Also, some people talk with dead relatives, and I think that's fine; they'll tell you sometimes what it's like on the other side and some wonderful things are shared like that, but as far as becoming guides, it's not a good idea, because they usually don't know a lot more than you do. And then, if you continue talking with them for a long time, that slows them back from doing what they need to do on the other side, as it can slow you from doing what you need to do."

One of the best ways to keep your connections on higher levels is to raise your vibrations, Jenny said, and there are a number of methods for doing so.

"First of all, let your energy run down in your body and then you see how heavy you feel. Then, ask your energy to run up in your body and you feel lighter. Floating. Any time you're floating that raises your vibration. Use prayer for protection. Prayer raises your vibration. Some people like certain kinds of music, meditation, or classical music that lifts them up, that raises their vibrations."

Jenny also suggests the simple yet powerful technique of filling the aura with love and light.

Evolution and Connecting with Higher Spiritual Dimensions

Jenny believes her own good guides to be from very high vibratory levels. She is familiar with those referred to in esoteric literature as the Ascended Masters, and she has had a sense of working with some among their ranks. On the other hand, she is resistant to labeling. Just because someone claims to be in contact with the Ascended Masters, does not mean it is so.

"I do think there is something to that [the Ascended Masters] and to the Great White Brotherhood. I do think [however], there's a lot of almost hokey stuff around it by some groups."

Still, she feels in its "pure form" the idea of a group of highly evolved beings that guide humanity is very accurate. On the other side, they work in their own departments and have varying levels of authority, and they assist us accordingly. (The word *white* is a reference to light, as race is not a factor.)

"It's like there's a system over there, and all have their purposes down to water sprites and gnomes and fairies. They all have their different things they do. Each has their own gifts, whether you're in the body or out of the body."

Jenny Ellen believes that the day will come when humanity as a whole will have a conscious awareness of working with other dimensions.

"That would come with natural evolution," Jenny said. "I think that's natural progression ... As more people evolve, then more people will be aware of them [in other dimensions]. It's like the same thing will be true then as now, it's just that more people will be involved and can comprehend it. I think the point I'm trying to make is, *they're* not changing [on the other side]; they're not manifesting more ... Humans are [changing].

"As you grow and develop, all sorts more things open up, more skills, more recognition of things. And it's like it was always there. It's like parallel dimensions. That stuff was always there, and then somebody discovered it—but they haven't discovered it, as far as the world goes, they just happened on to it."

Jenny sees conscious contact with higher spiritual dimensions expanding in the not-too-distant future, as many predictions have proclaimed. She is in accord with the Hopi Indians and other sources that predict major changes with the year 2012, which is the date when the Ancient Mayan calendar ends.

"I think that's going to be one of the big things with the 2012 thing," Jenny Ellen said. "We open so dramatically to other dimensions, to other realities, and each person will make quantum leaps from where they are. A person who's already developed a lot now will make a huge leap, but a person not very developed will make a huge leap too—it's just from where they start. If somebody's on the third floor and somebody's on the eighth floor, and you all go up four more levels, it's like each one has gained.

"And then the other thing is, let's say a person who might be on a third level might all of a sudden become so interested and open so much and really go with it, that their growth may end up being six levels instead of four, where somebody who is on a higher level might say, 'Oh, okay,' and just scarcely use the four levels they went up."

She gets a little fired up at the idea of it.

"That happens too many times to people who develop: They think they've arrived. They've gotten a lot of skills and abilities and just figure that they've arrived. And we don't *ever* arrive as such. Enlightenment has many levels. And if you run into somebody who knows it all, who has all the answers, they probably do, for the level in which they're operating, but that doesn't mean they would on [still] higher levels."

As for her, one gets the sense that she does not ever accept that *she* has arrived. She seems to be aware of being on an ongoing journey, while in good company.

Prayer continues to be a part of her existence.

"Prayer has always been a part of my life and not necessarily formal prayers. More spontaneous," she said.

She ruminated a bit.

"I do try to exercise," she said, then added, "always feel I should do more."

She tries to bring humor into life.

"I like to find some humor every day, or just to find humor in my body. Laughter is so healthy for the body, for the system."

To keep herself on course with the on high, she tunes in.

"I stop and tune into higher energies, feel uplifted, and feel good," Jenny Ellen said. "I look at pictures, appreciate pets, look out the window and get into a moment of something outside of myself, and let it lift me into the spiritual."

They are small things, perhaps. Adornments to a secret life.

Judith MacKenzie Castell
Daughter of Nova Scotia, Scribe of the Divine

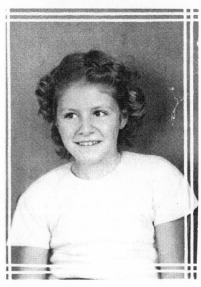

J udith MacKenzie Castell is a youthful sixty-seven-year-old who often steps into a sense of fun. On most days she moves with ease in white tennis shoes and blue jeans. She has a spring to her step and a joy that bubbles up, unbidden.

Like the skies of her native Nova Scotia that change with passing sea breezes, Judith moves in mood and thought with what comes and soon passes. In casual conversation she is mercurial, owning whatever the moment brings before it elapses. She loves a good laugh when it arrives, pains with old hurts remembered, and sighs with regrets recalled. And then, she moves on with the next moment.

Judy did not come easily to the work of offering intuitive guidance to others professionally. Her life was half lived before she dared publicize her services, much less muster the courage to charge for them.

The first time she ever charged for a psychic reading, she was terrified.

"I think I charged twenty [dollars], and my heart was pounding through every bit," she recalled. "And you know what I was challenged with? She had been to another psychic and was told the opposite. I said, 'Let's do something. Let's wait and see. I feel certain that after all these years my guides wouldn't steer me wrong.'" (Judy was correct in the matter, it turned out.)

As with many of the better intuitives, Judy has a conscious awareness of working with unseen guides from higher dimensions. One of the most striking things about her work is the crystalline clarity of the information she receives from these unseen helpers. In written intuitive readings, Judy transcribes her guides' dictation word for word, in answer to questions posed by clients. Or, if a client has no question, Judy relies on her steadfast prayer that the seeker be given what is most needed at that time. Her guides refer to her, in fact, as their scribe.

As such, she is an exacting scribe. She hears only two or three words at a time, and she writes them fast and furiously, putting them down precisely as they come—and if she unwittingly fails to do so, her spiritual helpers correct her. In fact, if she fails to transcribe the information just as they give it to her, they will not continue, she said. The dictation comes so piecemeal, that often Judy doesn't know the gist of what's being given until after it's written down. Then she goes over it and adds structure and punctuation. Many times she marvels at what comes through and has often ruminated, "Why can't I think of something like that?"

The process is not so-called automatic writing; rather it's listening clairaudiently. Clairaudience is defined as the ability to hear something that is beyond the physical senses.

Surprisingly, Judy—who can offer such stunningly clear guidance to others—has long had a hard time with her own self-confidence. It may be that this struggle is, in part, to help keep the ego out of the way. She said one thing that can interfere with her getting clear guidance is if her own opinion gets in the way.

"That's what I have to be concerned about," Judy explained, "fear that I'll mess up someone's life. There's a possibility of it when you involve yourself, when you overcome what's coming through, by your own opinion."

Unusual Experiences, to a Sense of the Divine

Nova Scotia is a province off the eastern coast of Canada and remains in many ways a far-flung vestige of settlers once homesick for the motherland. *Nova Scotia* means New Scotland, and the peninsula is peppered with her ancestors. In Judy is a genuine daughter of Scotland, for both her parents were Scottish. True to the Scots' reputations, both were fierce and thrifty.

In some respects, Judy has come full circle, for she is back to living in the house where she was born, her duties to her now-deceased parents fulfilled.

Most certainly, Judy's early background did not appear to support her giving intuitive or psychic readings.

"I was brought up in an evangelical church, [taught] that all this was of the devil," she said, and then she paused before quietly adding, "I realized it's divine, not of the devil."

When Judy was a small child, she heard her name being called though no one was there. She also had experiences of leaving her body and visiting other school children, where she could see them as well as what they were doing. When a cow went missing in the spring, she told her parents where it could be found, and there it was. Other unusual experiences followed, all generally dismissed by Judy's parents and her playmates, and for a long time even by herself.

Since her many unusual childhood experiences tended to be looked at askance by family members and others in the community, she put them away for a number of years.

"I was astral traveling up until the time I was ten years old. I told a neighbor kid, 'I saw you ... you got a spanking last night.' He said, 'You didn't see me.' I said, 'Yes I did, you were in the bedroom and this and that happened. He told the other kids and they said, 'You're weird.'

"I just thought everybody did that. I quit until later in life ... in my thirties."

Astral traveling occurs when the consciousness leaves the body in spirit.

"Being an only child, you had no one to talk to. I had a lot of time alone," Judy said.

When she was fourteen years old, Judy had a strange growth appear on her foot that frightened her. She prayed to God to heal it and promised that if God would heal her foot, she would serve God for the rest of her life. Her foot healed, and she has endeavored to keep that promise, though it hasn't always been easy or in ways that she might have expected.

Guided to Truth in a Spiritual Experience

It concerns Judy greatly that she not ever tell anyone anything in her readings that harms them. If that ever happened, she would quit.

"I'm like Edgar Cayce," Judy said, "If I ever found out that anything I said to anyone hurt them in any way, I would stop doing this."

Edgar Cayce is a running theme in Judy's spiritual life and is her inspiration in her work. Cayce was a rather reluctant prophet from Kentucky who began going into a trance—though at the time it was called sleeping—and giving genuinely useful information to others, such as healing remedies. Judy said many years ago she was directed to Cayce's teachings in a spiritual experience and told there was truth there. She sought information about him and, in doing so, found a place she could call home, spiritually, at least.

Reincarnation is a cornerstone of the Cayce teachings, but for much of Judy's life, it was not a part of her belief system.

"I wasn't exposed to it, really," she said. "But I was in Switzerland with my husband, and I just started crying and crying and didn't know why and he said, 'Maybe you had a past life here.'"

After that, and with the Cayce teachings as guidance, Judy began to explore the possibility of reincarnation and eventually came to embrace it wholeheartedly.

"It was the missing piece," she said.

Her now ex-husband helped open her to the metaphysical side of her life.

"My husband was a research scientist, and he had some of this [ability] himself," she said, "or I doubt that I'd be as open. He was a healer. His father was very deeply into Edgar Cayce, and he was a scientist as well.

"Everybody's in our life for a certain reason. We have lessons to teach or lessons to learn. We are all psychic. It's just developing it."

Search for God Study Group as a Springboard

After investigating and reading of and about Cayce in the 1980s, Judy began attending classes at the center Cayce and his followers founded in Virginia Beach, Virginia, the Association for Research and Enlightenment (ARE). Eventually, she hosted an ARE-sponsored

Search for God study group in her home. She held weekly sessions there from 1985 to 1992. Those meetings were where it was first suggested to Judy that she should offer to give readings to the public.

"The members of the group encouraged me," she said. "I gave readings all my life to people, I just didn't know it. I heard information to give them. The members of the group encouraged me to go public. I would interpret dreams for them. They pushed, because I was terrified … like Cayce, I was scared I would ruin someone's life.

"I was giving readings all along to the Cayce group," she said. "I'd hear inside, 'Say this …' It wasn't from me."

Judy has heard things, known things, seen things, and otherwise had paranormal experiences since she was a child.

"When I was a kid I knew instinctively what was wrong with someone," Judy recalled. "My parents would talk about what was wrong with someone, and I would try to tell them, to help, and they would say, 'What do you know about it? You get outside and play.'

"If I'm reading for you, the pictures come. It's like I have an inner world that's a replication of the outer world. In my mind's eye I'm seeing the scene I'm explaining. Like with my students, they'd come in for [career] training, and I'd see where I was going to place them. Like one girl I was counseling, I saw her in a nursing home and I said, 'Susie, have you ever thought about being a nurse?' 'Oh,' she said, 'I've always wanted to be a nurse.'

"I hear things, sense things, and see things. I have seen auras [the energy field around the body], but I don't have to, as I sense the aura … I sense moods, feelings, colors, pain. I'm clairsentient" (which means clear feeling or sensing).

Judy said although she can and does advise others based on her guidance, she acknowledges that ultimately, we all have free will.

"It boils down to people make their own choices," she said.

Duties as a Scribe

Judy sought to explain what being a scribe is like for her.

"I write the word as I hear it," she said. "I hear two or three words ahead … The practice is to shut up and listen."

Judy hears two or three words ahead of what she is writing. As she writes those down, she hears two or three more. She said sometimes she is stunned at the lucidity and originality of what comes through.

"I read them and say, 'Did this come through me? How could it have? I wasn't even thinking that.'"

She clearly has a reverence for those she works with in this other realm.

"They use so many words, but get to it [answering the question] in a beautiful way. It comes through without punctuation."

Judy playfully moans about the long roundabout way her guides sometimes have of getting to the answer of a question in a reading, revealing a playful interaction. More than once she refers to the circumspect way they have of answering questions. To many, however, this is one of the beautiful aspects of the readings. She describes the clever and circuitous manner her guides have of being able to tell a client what they need to hear, and then returning to the matter of the question asked, which may actually seem almost inconsequential by then.

Judy said her guides use this roundabout way of answering a client's question in order to seize the opportunity to give the client needed information. Judy's prayer before each reading is that the client be given what they need.

She said when she prays, she asks on behalf of the client, "that what they need to know be given to them, that the information will be for their highest good, and that they will be able to feel whatever they came with, in question of, or wanting to know, or just where they are in life, will be answered."

Judy has been tested in a scientific laboratory and was found to have the ability to move to a deeper level of consciousness within a matter of seconds. She suspects that, in her intuitive readings, she is accessing another, higher level of consciousness, another dimension. She does not ask for the name of any individual that may be working with her, as she has the sense that she is in communication with something beyond an individual consciousness.

"I believe it's a Collective Consciousness," she said. "The Great White Brotherhood is a name for the energy."

Judy sought to describe the experience of making contact with this level of consciousness.

"It's like an umbrella," she said. "I feel like when I go into the levels, it's like a doughnut with a hole that I go through, or they come down and surround me. Or I rise to them and meet them halfway. They know when it's finished [the session], and it's like they fold up the umbrella. It's like the umbrella sitting on the top of my head and they're channeling this information from there. Rays of information come down. It's transported back and forth. My energy goes up with the question, and theirs comes down with the answer.

"When I start to get the ego in it, it forms a little block, and they can't get their energy in," Judy said, explaining why, when she starts injecting her own opinion, the flow of exchange ceases.

"When a person goes into their authentic self, they don't let the ego bother them."

Judy now has an ease about this voice of sorts from beyond, though it unsettled her some when it first arrived.

"I don't fear them whatsoever," Judy said. She dismisses the notion of struggle. "Things should come easy."

In Touch with Sources from Higher Levels

Some say that Judy is in touch with sources from the upper vibratory levels of the spirit world. It is said that there are those on the other side who are guides to humanity, and among these is the so-called Great White Brotherhood of Ascended Masters. Judy signs her written readings "Great White Brotherhood of Ascended Masters" or "GWB," and sometimes adds "and Judy."

Judy first learned of the Great White Brotherhood at ARE and later from the Rosicrucians, an older metaphysical group that she was a member of. She recalls when she first heard mention of the Ascended Masters.

"I was at ARE and something was said about the Great White Brotherhood. I just had a quickening within and I thought, 'What's this all about?' Then I felt very drawn to the Rosicrucians, and they talk about the Great White Brotherhood.

"Whenever I hear the name [Great White Brotherhood], it's just like a warm loving feeling goes through me ... I give people information and I think, *Isn't that wonderful. How come I can't think of something like that?*"

When asked who she knows the Great White Brotherhood to be, Judy said, "People who have trodden the world, and some of them who haven't had to come to the world, and they have come ... like a Senate, to help people."

The Ascended Masters are said to be a perfected group of beings, some of whom learned their life lessons through a series of incarnations, yet who pledged to remain nearby, to help guide humanity from the spirit world. Some of the Ascended Masters have not needed to incarnate on earth, because it was not necessary for their learning or development or their ability to be of assistance to humanity. Some say these masters do God's bidding, in accordance with God's laws and man's and, therefore, always with respect for mankind's free will.

Asked how her contact with the GWB first began, Judy said they started coming to her through her writings.

"It scared me at first," Judy recalled, "because I thought, 'Is this like a negative entity?' But there was so much love around it, and I thought of the Christ energy and it didn't leave and it didn't change.

"I had this thing I had to write—all of a sudden it came out 'ye' and 'thee,' and it was a different consciousness. I was reading it to [my friend] Marge and I said, 'I'm getting these messages ... '

"I would listen within and hear ... 'Have ye ever thought it might be like this...' It's like a blackboard television in my mind. That's how I use it in my work. I'm given different angles to consider."

When asked why it is that her guides use archaic English words in their writings such as *ye* and *thee*, Judy said simply, "It distinguishes them."

Sometimes, however, Judy feels she's not to know certain things.

"If I get a no from them, I feel like I'm not to know," she said.

Other times, she questions her guides, playfully. Theirs is a true friendship—one developed over time and built on trust, a genuine relationship in which she interacts with these unseen guides, arguing a point here, objecting there, teasing, yet always acquiescing because, ultimately, experience has taught her the wisdom of doing so, as her guides always turn out to be right. It is a loving relationship. In fact, she says, simply, sincerely, "I love them."

Everyday Life Lived with a Twist

Judy enjoys playing music with local fellow musicians. She checks out yard sales with her girlfriends. She goes to dances with them. She writes. She talks on the phone with her daughter and new grandson, who live in the States. She checks in on family, chats with the neighbors, and pets her cats. She has no particular daily spiritual practice that she observes to keep herself attuned.

"It's just like I'm in communication all the time," Judy said. "It's just like I'm open. It's just like, 'Well, God, what are we going to do today?' It's like an awareness around me all the time."

Sometimes, however, Judy feels a need to withdraw and restore herself to herself.

"It's like I get so filled up with the vibrations of society that I have to have a week or two to get myself straightened out. I pick up energy very subtly anyway. It's like my aura gets full."

Being a sensitive, sometimes Judy feels things and then has to ascertain whose it is or what it's about.

"I close myself off if I feel people's vibes coming to me, like ripples of fear coming to me, and I'll realize someone could be thinking of me or I'll say, 'Okay, who is it?'

"I'll just scan my friends to see if I can pick up anything. If there's anybody dying, I get a really terrible feeling. I did that with the [twin] towers [9/11]. I was so depressed two days before [they went down]. It's like, 'Please, if anyone … ?' After I tell it to people [usually] I'm free. It's like someone knocking on my head."

Judy said if she feels something and it seems to be a presence, then 95 percent of the time she's picking up the vibes of someone in her soul group or her friends or relatives.

For instance, she told of a time when she felt a sense of dread go through her, and then she "scanned" her friends and relatives to see if they were all right. Still uncertain about what the source of the feeling was—or maybe because of it—she called her friend Linda.

"I said, 'Are you all right?' She said, 'Yeah.' I said, 'Is Ken [Linda's husband] all right?' She said, 'Well, he doesn't feel very well.' I said, 'Tell him to get to the doctor quick' because my readings are always preventative. I said, 'If he doesn't get to the hospital by ten o'clock tonight, he'll be dead.'"

Linda, who was sitting nearby as Judy related the tale, chimed in.

"We had four feet of snow," Linda recalled. "They had to get a snowmobile to get him out [of their area], and still he barely made it. He fell off once, and the paramedics started working on him before he even got put in the ambulance."

Ken survived.

Judy said local people come up to her frequently and tell her that things she once predicted came true, often years after their reading. She said they'll say, "Aren't you that fortune teller from out at Hilden?"

"Yep," she answers, not objecting to the old, not always positively associated moniker, for she has learned to take lightly that which once stung.

She has run across former clients who have said such things as, "You told me three years ago that I'd go back with my ex-husband, and I didn't believe you, but we're getting married tomorrow."

This confirmation pleases her.

Early Days of Psychic Exploration

Judy reflected on the early days of her psychic work and exploration and on the shroud surrounding it.

"You had to be quiet about what you did [back then]," she said. "You're talking about what we older ones went through, being called weirdos and all. They told us that we were in the clutches of Satan and that they were praying that I wouldn't die, because they didn't want me to die while I was in Satan's clutches.

"I went to a spirit-themed event at a church once, and I was all excited, and the priest said to me, 'Unless you denounce all this [metaphysical work], you'll have to leave.' I said, 'You're asking me to give up the promise I made [to God]. I can't do that.' I left in tears."

Judy continued to offer intuitive guidance to others because she truly believes this guidance comes from divine levels. Had she thought about it, she might not have considered that she was someone whom divine guidance would come through, yet with her gentle and loving innocence that often shows, it fits that she would be suited for this work.

"When I was married, my husband was a scientist, and we would go to these meetings, and they were all educated and wanted to know where I got my degree. I told them I didn't have any degree, that I had a degree in the School of Hard Knocks! And I laughed. When I taught life skills (later) I understood. Otherwise I wouldn't have known how they felt." She drops her head then lifts it again. Judy later took university courses and trained for her teacher's license and her experiences helped her counsel those she worked with.

"There's always a plan ... I grew up very poor. Everything I wanted, I had to cry for it. I would get in trouble at school for not having my Scribblers [writing pad], but then my dad wouldn't give me the money for it."

Judy said, before the end of his life, her father came to appreciate that she gave intuitive readings to people and gave credence to her work.

"He would never say much about what I did, but just before he died, he said, 'Judy, you got the gift from me.' He didn't dare say anything [before] because the family was evangelical."

She said her father was what is now known as a horse whisperer.

"He could do anything with a horse," she said quietly, remembering.

Judy's mother also gradually accepted the fact that Judy gave psychic readings, and she came to embrace Judy's work before she passed in 2000. Judy said her mother became quite interested in the Rhine [psychic] studies conducted at Duke University and often read about them.

"Mum was quite taken with my ability," Judy recalled. "She was about eighty then. She got used to a lot of things in the last three or four years of her life. The veil [to the other side] is thinner then. And she would see things I said come true."

However, back when Judy first started giving readings publicly, there were serious objections from other members of the family and from some in the community.

"I didn't want it to get back to my aunt [what I was doing] ... and I was at the post office and a lady said, 'A group of us and your aunt are praying for you.'"

Judy bristles, even now as she remembers it. "I said, 'My understanding of prayer is the person must want it ... otherwise it won't be effective.' See, that was mind power, mind control of fifteen people. I kind of had it hard at first."

Judy's remaining family is more accepting now, including the aunt just referred to. That aunt is eighty-eight years old and lives near Judy. They are friends, and Judy often cares for her. Still, no one in her family would go to Judy for a reading.

"Phffft!" she said, laughing at the very thought of it. "Nobody will listen to me. My cousin ... had welts break out. I had to get up out of bed and write a letter [a reading for him] ... He rented a building where a mosquito repellent was formulated and bottled. My writing had depicted that the building still contained a high amount of the chemicals used and this contributed to my cousin's condition.

"A so-called prophet is not known in her own home town. But something came out [in that letter], and it's not from me."

From ARE Study Group to Field-Tested Psychic

Judy and her friend Marge, a local postmaster, remember their ARE study group, the members of which eventually prompted Judy to offer to give readings to others.

The two women recalled some successes that their group had.

"We had people come from all over to have us do healing sessions," Judy said. "We had sessions of looking for people who were lost, locating lost articles, and we did healings on each other ... After some of the healing sessions, people would call and say, 'The doctor can't find anything.'"

When questioned about the eventual demise of such a group, Marge and Judy agreed, "It was like it was time for it to end ... Everyone who came in got what they came for. We tried another group [later], but it didn't flow. People went on [with it] as an individual thing."

When asked if she still gets readings from Judy, Marge the postmaster replied, "All the time. Her accuracy in her readings is high, 90 percent—at least I think it is—sometimes she's not quite so sure."

Judy is on ARE's list of field-tested, recommended psychics. She was a staff psychic for ARE's Developing Your Intuition class in Virginia Beach for several years. She reads differently for those people and the ones who write to her because they are usually interested in their spiritual growth. In fact, Judy feels her readings are strongest in spiritual counseling.

Locals, however, still want a fortune teller.

"People in my area are looking for a fortune teller; they're not as interested in spiritual growth. They want the cards and runes [prophetic stones]. Then, I use the Major Arcana of the Tarot deck; it sums it up. Remember, with certain people, if I don't have props, they just think … that I'm making it up."

Usually, locals think Judy needs *something* in order to get information for them, from a deck of playing cards to tea leaves, which she reads. She does begin each reading for locals with a written message from the Great White Brotherhood. The writing lists topics for her to zero in on, from messages from deceased relatives, on. Then, she interprets the runes and the Tarot.

In interpreting what arises symbolically, such as what's seen in the tea leaves, Judy simply knows what the object is intended to represent. For instance, a client reported seeing a picture during meditation that he couldn't figure out. It was a flash in his mind's eye of flowers in the middle of his driveway. He asked Judy what this might mean. Without missing a beat, she asked, "How do you drive yourself?" The client admitted to a history of pushing himself very hard, of being a bit of a workaholic.

"I do that with tea leaves," Judy explained, "as soon as I see something there, my mind automatically knows what it is."

Marge remembered the start of Judy's intuitive career. "I said, 'You should start doing readings and charge for them. Once it started, we [the ARE study group] were the guinea pigs and let her do it as often as she wanted to in order for her to do what she was meant to do, as far as I'm concerned."

Judy said two years ago, at the last minute, she didn't go to ARE to give readings during their intuitive training class because the guidance she received in a dream steered her away from doing so.

"You've got to be smart enough to listen," Marge interjected.

Judy's beloved dog of many years died days later. Had she gone to ARE, she would have been away when he passed, which would have been a source of great sadness for her. The dog was a special gift from a friend, long since deceased. Judy has had many experiences with her friend since his death. In fact, she feels so strongly about life after death that she would like to teach about it and is writing a book based on her experiences.

Readings Preceded by Prayer and Carried Out in Faith

Judy's relationship with the Great White Brotherhood is built on trust and calls for it in order to proceed. But there's a teasing, perhaps pretend skepticism, that surfaces because sometimes Judy challenges them. It would be a dull affair if she was only their scribe and there was no loving interaction, no playfulness, and no humor.

In the end, though, she gets her opinion out of the way and offers up what is given.

"I have to go with what I get," she said. If they offer it, she conveys it.

A case in point is found in the first sentence of another reading Judy gave, in which the GWB told her to use a word she'd never heard of. She argued about it. They insisted. She tried to look it up in the dictionary and couldn't find it. In the end, she used the word anyway, for that is her level of trust.

The suggested word was *vicissitudes*. The reason Judy couldn't find it in the dictionary was because she was spelling it as *vistitudes*. She put the word in the reading anyway, even while not knowing what it meant or if it existed as a word. They gave it, and she felt correct about conveying what was given, and did so.

The client in question had asked about the wisdom of buying a second home. As the GWB dictated and Judy transcribed, they responded: "As we find the lass in the vistitudes of self-indulgence a wee bit, we would ask her what the heart is saying?"

Judy sent the reading to the client, and then discussed it with her by phone. She asked the client if she knew that word, which Judy pronounced correctly. The client assured her that she did.

"What's it mean?" Judy asked.

"Ups and downs," the client replied and told Judy that the use of the word was appropriate. When the client looked at the written reading, however, she realized that Judy had misspelled it and explained to Judy why she had been unable to locate the word.

Even as Judy did not know the word and was unable to find it in the dictionary, she used it. Why? Because her relationship with the GWB developed over the years and is built on trust, ever since the GWB first began coming to her consciously in the 1980s.

"In my writings [journaling] I had thought, 'Why is this like this or that?' and then they would just come through. Like, [writing] about 'Where am I going in life?' they would break in, 'Yes, our child, as we see it …' or 'From where we are …'"

When asked if she meditates to get her information, Judy said, "I meditated when I was a little kid. When I first went to ARE and they started talking about meditation, I thought, 'Good heavens, I must be doing something wrong because I'm not doing it that way.'

"I could always be in touch with the spirit world. I believe I was a meditative person all my life … I was put on biofeedback machines and told I could go to deeper levels in six seconds. It's part of my life and who I am."

To best describe the meditative side of Judy, it may be helpful to refer to a reading she gave in which the client asked for advice regarding meditation. Judy the scribe and her guides wrote the following:

> *We would suggest ye go on a journey. As our scribe [Judy] sits here typing we have asked that she look out her window and describe what is going on around her … a meditation she often does, although she doest not realize it as meditation, until now, as we speak. She will write what she is experiencing.*

Judy then wrote:

> *As I sit in my chair at the computer the hum of the refrigerator in the kitchen plays a rhythm in the background, joining the singing sound of the computer. They seem to be in a harmonic symphony of rhythm and sound—all their own. As I raise my eyes to the living room window I see the tall Wild Buckwheat plants waving at me from the outside of the window, are gently tossed back and forth by the wind. They also sing to me. A symphony of sound, the melodious wind joins the fridge and computer as a background, sounds of soothing contentment and joy to be alive. The plants' greenery—life itself. A gust of wind suddenly flips the leaves over and yet they sing forth, never missing a beat, a most beautiful gusty song. My heart is feeling the love of life with the sun shining upon the underneath side of the plants' leaves as they toss to and fro. The blue sky as a background gives them the appearance of singing and dancing to an inner rendition of their own song. I feel peace. I feel love. I feel joy. I say a prayer of Gratitude. I send out thoughts of love and healing to the Universe and all its people. I send out thoughts of love and healing to the universes unseen. The intake of breath slowly raises my chest and the exhale of breath slowly lowers my chest. I listen to my breathing—in and out, in and out—I am a child of the Oneness of all ... a child of the universe ... all that is ... .I am one with the Universe ... I am one with my Creator ... I am one with myself. I am that I am.*

As for the rest of the answer to the meditation question posed by the client, they continued:

> *We would suggest ye not let distraction of sound make thee ill at ease so as not to meditate. Let sound be a positive, a vehicle to bring ye to a deeper awareness of thy oneness with all. In this world of thine, ye are becoming more and more surrounded by sound. Let thy memories of thy Nature Spirits and helpers bring to thee thy re-acquaintance of thy*

love and joy of thy nature sounds so that ye may combine such with thy exterior worldly sounds. Combined, ye may change these vibrations to accommodate ye for thy purpose and reduce thy inner constant mind chatter. Listen to this and thy breathing. Become one with thy breath and know that this life force energy is helping ye to renew each cell within thy body, bringing health and balance to ye in all areas of thy body, mind and spirit.

"In giving readings," Judy said, "I'm in a state of nothingness. When I get a reading, I read the questions, and I just go blank and then let any impressions sink in, and I might jot them down so when I go sit down to do the reading, I'll have it there. Then I'll check what I jotted down. The answer may veer off, and then I'll wonder and look back to make sure I answered the question."

She said sometimes it's like finding the space between breaths.

"Other times, it's different. I just lead from within. I just go with the flow. When I'm ready to do the readings, everything in my life is going like this." She holds out a hand, level and steady, "a nice even flow. I don't push to do the reading until I'm in the calm, in my meditative state. I wait until I hear the inner voice saying, 'Okay, it's time to do this reading' [for those reading requests mailed in].

"It's like now; I'm in that calm loving feeling."

Judy said it's easier to be in touch with her guides at night because mass consciousness is at rest.

"There will be nights when I can't sleep, and they [her guides] say that they want me to get up and do a reading, and I finally get up [and do it], and then I lay back down and go to sleep, bang. They'll come out with things I never even thought of.

"Our internal discussions are really our guides."

Generally, Judy won't give readings if she has other things to tend to, or simply isn't feeling strong. History has taught her useful lessons about giving too much of herself away.

"I don't like to read when I'm not well," she said.

A Past of Highs and Lows

Despite the clear intuitive guidance Judy can offer others, her life has not been without difficulties. On the other hand, she has had a variety of accomplishments. She counts among them the time she drove a school bus and successfully negotiated Nova Scotia's long and snowy winters. She liked the challenge and interacting with the kids.

She also recalls heady days. At one point she gave readings in Halifax, the capital of the province. She gave readings in a bookstore—sometimes as many as fifteen a day—without tiring. She remembers those days fondly.

"When I was in Halifax, I was really accurate, I thought. I gave readings in a bookstore from 1993 to 1996 ... Even if they [clients] didn't ask the questions, I'd sense what they were going to ask. Pictures came, snap snap. I was right on then. The readings energize me, unless my energy is gone.

"I had to give up readings in 1996. I was exhausted and sick ... I had fibromyalgia ... *Candida* ... I got sick and had to sell my home ... I was mad at God ... It was the midnight of the soul."

Judy is referring to what is often mentioned in spiritual literature as the "dark night of the soul." It is looked on as a test for spiritual seeker, and may be a time when others seem to turn away. God, the Source Itself, seems to withdraw. There have been other such tests, Judy said.

"In 1996 [after getting sick], I thought, 'Why do my guides desert me?' When, really, it was me not eating right. And, it was *Candida*."

Judy talks a lot about *Candida*, which she feels is chronic in modern times, causing serious complications for many. *Candida* is an excess of yeast in the system and can be brought about by eating sugars, starches that turn to sugar, grains, imperceptible molds on certain foods, dairy products, and antibiotics. In pregnant and nursing women, *Candida* is passed to infants, contributing to untold problems such as chronic ear infections and is what Judy sees as a possible cause of some cases of autism. Judy also thinks heavy multiple immunizations administered to very small children may cause autism in some instances.

Also, Judy thinks the way we deal with newborns in modern times can cause them difficulties.

"The way babies are taken from their mothers and whisked away and poked for blood and tests and left alone screaming and crying—it sends a shock to the system," she said.

Illness and poverty have returned to Judy's life more than once, including fairly recently.

"I'm just getting back into it, psychic work. I've been working through hardships with the readings ... In July, before skin cancer came on, I was really frustrated and didn't know which way to turn.

"I would sit and meditate so I would bring myself out of my body and be beyond my pain; then I could do the reading. But if I was tired ... I couldn't do it at that time.

"It's just like now; I'm in that peaceful loving feeling ...

"I took sick this time because I gave too much of myself away. I did a reading for myself, and they said I was pushing out too much.

"The Higher Powers really look after me. When they feel I'm ready to do a reading, the phone rings. It's like the Universe says, 'Our scribe is not in a condition mentally, physically, or emotionally to do a reading.'

"But when I feel like I do today, 'Okay, but don't swamp her.'"

When asked about doing readings for herself, Judy can do it, but, "I just don't like what they tell me at times. They pressure me and say very nicely, 'If you would but listen.'"

Test on the Path

Asked if she ever had a sense of breaking through a veil, or if the other side was always open to her, Judy tells a story.

"I was attacked in my home by an entity," she said, and then hesitated and her voice dropped. "I don't want to scare people," she said, and after a pause continued.

"It went bang from the closet door, and the cat jumped on the bed. All of a sudden up the hall the radio came on. I thought, 'How did that come on?' I walked out of the kitchen and got a cold blast on my arm, and I said, 'Oh, we've got an entity here do we.' The lights wouldn't come on, so I crossed myself and asked for protection. It was ten after four [a.m.], and all of a sudden—bang! This man came out of the closet and laid across me … He said he was going to have his way with me. I said, 'My Lord will protect me.' He said, 'There's no such thing.'

"I looked out the window and started singing, 'My God will protect me …' I was terrified. I recited the Lord's Prayer. But after he went, there was such a feeling of love and protection … I was soaking wet where he'd laid on me …

"Later, [author] Marilyn Rosner said I'd just passed a spiritual test …"

Judy gained something profound from the unusual experience.

"I had to learn the peace which passeth all understanding," she said.

In assorted books on mysticism and in Mary Gray's *The Gateway of Liberation*, this type of experience is discussed as one of the tests that sincere spiritual seekers must pass, when the light is called on, so that a spiritual seeker is not hampered by a fear of dark forces.

Trusting Her Guidance in Spite of Doubts

When people read their written readings from her, different parts will jump out at them at different times, according to Judy's guides. Perhaps this is in keeping with Judy's prayer that people be given what they need to know at that time.

Judy's guides sought to give one client what he needed to know in a reading. The man, unbeknownst to Judy, had changed his name from a common one to a rather unusual one, at the suggestion of a former so-called guru. This was not mentioned in his questions; however, Judy's reading put forth this message:

> *Yes, we have Kevock Braeward, as he is called … We would suggest … that ye might consider a name change around ye … for we see an incompatibility within thy name … What have ye done with thy name? One [name] going against the other so to speak … one draining upon the other. This change has dispelled energy from thy "Intent" and doest not vibrate with thy purpose and goal, therefore ye feel a wall go up, so to speak, regarding applying self to "giving thy all" [the client had asked about feeling he was not giving his all in his work]. What hast been done?*

> *Ask self. Why hast thou changed/added to that already given ye at thy birth by thy parents, whom were pressed upon by Higher Powers to name thee? What has ye done in consideration of another to thy name?*

Judy described some of what she went through when doing the reading for "Kevock" whom she had never met or talked to.

Judy said when she first approached the reading, she thought, "Ugh that name … Ooh … I thought it could be me, but what it was was the Ascended Masters were already there, giving me an impression … I thought, 'My God, if this is wrong, this is going to take him down another path of insecurity and hard knocks.'

"There was such a strong feeling that I couldn't shake no matter how many times I got up from the computer and walked around the house, confused in what was coming through regarding his name … Adopted? Changed? Something to do with name change, which has an effect upon his life to do with the vibrations that surround he and his activity … It really stumped me, the scribe. So I wrote down what the Ascended GWB Masters bid me do and let go of my query. I had never run into this before when doing a reading. I prayed that he would know what the Masters were referring to and that it was helpful to him."

Judy was correct that this gentleman had done something with his name. Even as it made no sense to her, Judy trusted and went with the information she was given.

Contact with the Other Side Enriches Life

When Judy has temporarily lost her sense of contact with the other side, it has been difficult for her.

"I have been out of attunement with the voice [she hears], and I feel so alone. I feel lost and forlorn. I thought, 'If this is all there is, I don't want to be here.'"

Many people meditate, and some of them are reportedly in touch with the spirit world. Some even claim to be in touch with the Ascended Masters. But the clarity and the high level of Judy's contact and her accompanying ideals is perhaps what distinguishes and defines her and her work.

"I pattern my life after Christ," she said, adding, "By their fruits, ye shall know them."

Judy speaks of others with kindness. She has never had anyone show up for a reading that she didn't like and seemed surprised at the thought of it.

"That I didn't like?" she reiterated, "No, but sometimes I feel like I'm not supposed to read for someone. I may tell them I'm not feeling well or just can't read for them at that time. And sometimes someone will call for an appointment, and I'll just feel like I'm not supposed to read for that person."

Maybe this is her secret, the simplicity of her love, unclouded by judgment.

"What does it matter if others like you or not?" she said, "Love *them* to bits."

Catherine Rosek

Corporate Fixture to Seer

Catherine Rosek's voice belies her age. Although Cathy is in her mid-sixties, her voice has the lilt and uplifting resonance of a young woman's. Her silver hair surprises those who only know her by voice. It is a silver that sparkles.

Cathy does most intuitive readings by phone, so those who simply know her by the sound of her youthful and strong voice may wonder how someone so young can offer such penetrating insights. In intuitive sessions, she is, by turns, careful and excited. When ignited with the possibility of seeing something especially promising for the client, she can even be described as exuberant.

Yet there is a softness to Cathy Rosek's countenance, and a polite normalness. She is solicitous, with a pleasing laugh that arrives easily. She is cheerful and earnest. She chooses tea over coffee. Although by no means timid, there is a near shyness that attends her.

She keeps a tidy house with her husband, Bill, in an unassuming suburb of Colorado Springs—an area once considered largely conservative, which is actually in keeping with Cathy's background. She came from corporate America and an early home environment that did not entertain anything paranormal. That she is doing this work surprises even her. For years, she was very cautious about letting other people know she was doing "this weird, crazy thing."

One wonders, how did someone who was a housewife then a fixture of the corporate world become a seer?

Innocent Beginnings

It all started innocently enough. When Cathy and Bill married in 1969, nothing suggested that there would be anything unusual about their lives. They had never even discussed anything spiritual, Cathy said. Then, in the first year of their marriage, a friend loaned them the book, *There Is a River: The Story of Edgar Cayce* by Thomas Sugrue.

Cayce was a so-called prophet who, by going into deep trance gave a wealth of helpful information to others. All of the readings done by Cayce are on file at the center Cayce and supporters established known as the Association for Research and Enlightenment (ARE).

Cathy and Bill were prompted to investigate the Cayce legacy. They were so drawn to his teachings that they eventually joined a Search for God study group, based on steps Cayce recommended for such a group.

Bill and Cathy's lives would never be quite the same, but Cathy would long keep at bay such high drama as going into trance herself.

The Search for God study group activities included meditation. When Cathy first attempted to meditate in 1969, she struggled.

"As a part of the ARE study group—it met once a week—we ended each session with a meditation that was guided by the *Search for God* study book," Cathy recalled. "But I have to tell you that I had a very difficult time with that, because, first of all, my mind didn't want to get quiet, just like everybody else's doesn't want to get quiet.

"And then, the other thing about it [was], there were not enough directions: 'Still your mind.' Give me a break—that is *not* a good direction! So what I did was, I went out looking for tools that would help me, and what I found was not a book on meditation, but a book on concentration ... and I believe the idea was, you use a candle and you gaze at the flame until you became like one with the flame. And that's what got me there, because that's what got my mind to be quiet. I mean, it's very hypnotic to stare into a candle flame or a fire."

Cathy began to genuinely enjoy her meditations. Meanwhile, she and Bill became deeply involved in the study of dreams. They kept journals of their dreams and went to great effort to analyze and interpret them. In the early days, Cathy said the practice was like having her own personal psychologist.

"My dreams began to bring up issues for me," she said. "My dreams began to show me the things in my life that were blocking me, that were holding me back …

"We did dreams for ever and ever, and we got predictions through dreams and things like that," Cathy said. "Finally we determined that getting information through dreams is just way too cumbersome, because you have to interpret all these symbols. And at the same time, our meditations were giving us clearer guidance."

Once Bill and Cathy shifted their attention from dreams to meditation, they were just as intent in their focus.

"We both started meditating twice a day, every day, for fifteen minutes, before we went to work and fifteen minutes when we came home from work," Cathy said, then interjected, "Never meditate before you go to bed, because you fill yourself with so much energy that you probably aren't going to sleep. So meditate early in the evening or meditate during the day. Or a lot of people find meditating in the early morning, like somewhere between three and four or four-thirty is very good.

"It's a true fact that the veils [between realms of consciousness] are thinner at that time of every day … that's when the veils are thinner and that's when contact is easier. Now, once you really get moving with your meditation and everything, you don't need the veils to be thinner to make the contact. But a lot of people find that that's very effective for them."

When Cathy speaks of contact, she is referring to the spirit world and guides on the other side of the veils that hide the truth of higher realities.

Unspoken Experiences as a Child

As a child, Cathy had a few unusual experiences. When she played with others, for instance, she did not like to speak. In looking back, she believes she sensed that speaking "diminished the experience, that it took it down to a lower level."

She had imaginary playmates, but they were animals.

"You know, spirit playmates, not people," Cathy said. "They were always animals ... I talked to them; we played in the back yard."

She also had an ability to listen to people and to understand why they were failing to communicate effectively.

"As far back as I can remember, I can listen to people talk to each other, and I can understand why they're not communicating. I can see that one is talking at this level, one is talking at that level and never the twain shall meet."

Cathy also had some standout experiences, where time not only stood still, but seemed not to matter.

"I've had probably half a dozen experiences where I was just somewhere, like outside walking or something, and all of a sudden it was like time stopped and, yes, I was still there, but I was someplace else too," Cathy said. "And there were, like, tinkling bells and there was like this fairy dust, and I knew that those were very important experiences.

"I knew that they were experiences out of time and out of space, in other dimensions of consciousness, and they were basically for the purposes of getting my attention. They were wonderful. It's an awesome experience to have. Everything is so perfect. And there's nothing to disturb anything because it's totally still, because everything has stopped: time and space.

"So, my sense [is] that was actually [my] experiencing a state of *being*, a state of oneness with the soul, a state of oneness with spirit, being in this world and not of it in any way, for a brief period."

Cathy sighs in fond remembrance of those special experiences. And she remembers too, knowing, just knowing, not to mention any of it to her family.

"I was wise enough never to mention any of this," Cathy said. "I knew. Intuitively I knew: you don't go there with this. My family was Catholic, and my mother was basically thrown out of the church, well, not allowed to take communion, after she got divorced, and she and my grandparents moved to a Methodist church ...

"I never really understood that other people weren't having the same experience that I was having, but I never felt the need to talk about it, and it was the same feeling [as] when I was playing with someone and having to talk. It diminished the experience, it took it down, you know, to a lower level."

Seeking Guidance from Higher Realms

Cathy is among those who believe that higher spiritual realms exist and can be accessed. She also believes that life can be enriched by that awareness and subsequent contact. However, she herself was slow to cultivate such contact. She meditated, she studied, she prayed, but when it came to establishing relationships with unseen forces from other realms, she was afraid. And she left it at that for a very long time.

"It was April of 1989 ... when I finally got up the courage to let myself go into a trance state and meet my guides. I had been meditating [since 1969], and they had been trying to get [my attention] during my meditation. And other things were happening to try to get my attention, and I basically told them, 'Stop it. Leave me alone. I'm not doing this.' And for twenty years they left me alone.

"I'm talking about spirit and the guides. They left me alone for twenty years ... because I was terrified. I was totally terrified. The very idea ... What was happening was, I would be, like, washing dishes or something, and I would hear a voice very clearly calling my name."

Clairaudience is the ability to hear something outside the norm, beyond the physical senses.

Initially, Cathy did not welcome her ability to hear voices that were not "there."

"Finally I turned around one night, and I said, 'Look, you knock it off or I'm not even going to meditate anymore. We're not going to have any contact whatsoever.'"

Cathy didn't really mean it because she enjoyed her meditations too much to stop. She felt meditation was changing her life. Still, she had a deep-seated terror, which she and Bill would later explore. Meanwhile, she left the fear in place and only vaguely acknowledged an awareness of presences beyond the veils.

"I didn't even attempt to work through it. It was like, 'I'm meditating. I'm growing. This is working for me in my life. You guys go find somebody else. I'm not doing this ... ' So for twenty years

I didn't. Then what really happened was I had a situation in my life where someone I knew very well, someone who was very close to me, basically turned into an accident looking for a place to happen. And I prayed. I asked for guidance, 'How can I help?' … And basically, I know now that what my guides and angels said was, 'Gotcha.'"

As soon as she made the decision to explore contact with other realms of consciousness, Cathy was led to a book written by Sanaya Roman and Duane Packer called *Opening to Channel: How to Connect with Your Guide.* That book was instrumental in helping her, Cathy said.

"I started working with the book because it was the answer to my prayers … There was so much integrity in the book. I had so much faith and trust in the process and in the guide who was coming through Sanaya, and so it took me about two weeks to work through [it] and work up the courage to do the exercise where you actually meet your guides, and after I did that and my guide came in, I was like, 'So that's what all the fuss was about? You've gotta be kidding me … This is terrific.'

"But I didn't waste a lot of time on regret," she added, smiling.

Still, it took a while for Cathy to trust the information that was coming through her, mostly because it was coming through *her.*

"I didn't tell anybody for a while; I would do it upstairs in the bedroom," Cathy said. "I would try to talk into a tape recorder, and just—just keep everything in the closet. But once I shared it with my husband, and I did some channeling sessions for him where he was able to ask questions, he trusted it immediately and thought that I was crazy for being so concerned, being so worried, not believing it, not trusting it, et cetera et cetera.

"It actually took me probably a year, a year and a half … to start being willing to do it for other people. But I can't tell you when *I* started actually trusting it, because it was well down the road. I was like, 'Nope, I look in the mirror. I see me. I know me. This—nah, I don't trust this.'"

And she giggled.

"But Bill did. And he got some really good answers."

Bill, it turned out, would help lead Cathy to a belief in her guidance by needing it himself.

"We were living on our farm at the time," Cathy recalled. "One of the things that made me trust [the internal guidance] was, he came in one day and he was all agitated. He was working on the tractor, and he couldn't get it to run and he said, 'Sit down … I want to ask your guides what's wrong with this tractor.'

"Well, I, who know nothing about diesel engines and tractors and all that, sat down. The guide explained to him exactly what was wrong with the tractor, two different areas, what needed to be done. He went out, he did it. The tractor ran.

"And it was like, 'You know, you probably ought to start believing this.' So they've given me opportunities to believe, to trust."

A Belief in Reincarnation Comes Easily

Cathy said the occurrence with the tractor was one of the first incidents that nudged her to trust in the guidance coming through her. But she acknowledged that other, as yet unknown factors contributed to her protracted reluctance to actively engage that guidance.

"I think part of my not trusting it, too, was being unwilling to put myself out there, in jeopardy again, as I had in past lives, you know."

Bill and Cathy eventually found the origins of Cathy's fear in a past life where she was harmed for having such beliefs and engaging in such practices.

Early in her spiritual search, she incorporated a belief in reincarnation into her philosophy. Once she was exposed to it, acceptance came easily. She thinks this was in part because she had believed it in previous lives and that it was therefore a part of her soul makeup.

Cathy believes that we are each here to learn, to grow, and to evolve, and that life on earth is, in some ways, like a great play that we put on in order to act out events that will teach and test us.

Cathy said two books were instrumental in helping her to develop her belief system about reincarnation: *Radical Forgiveness, Making Room for the Miracle* by Colin Tipping helped her to gain insights, as did *Many Mansions: The Edgar Cayce Story on Reincarnation* by Gina Cerminara. In the early years of her search, she said the writings of Vera Stanley Alder helped to expand her philosophy.

Once Bill and Cathy's belief systems were open to reincarnation, that belief created a tapestry of understanding that helped to transform their lives.

Lightworkers Living with Difficulties

Cathy had not had a happy life growing up or a close relationship with her mother.

"It was quite poor," Cathy recalled. "My mother was actually married six times. In the beginning when I was very young, we basically lived in a ghetto in Savannah [Georgia] … and I had a very dysfunctional family. But you're going to find that most lightworkers have that story."

A lightworker is someone who sheds light where there is darkness. Cathy believes her difficult childhood was purposeful, because, unless a lightworker who counsels others has gone through difficult times, she may not understand others who come before her for guidance.

Many of us are faced with resolving old conflicts, and that process is part of a clearing that needs to go on in order that we might move to higher levels of consciousness. She believes that the ascension, that is sometimes spoken of by spiritually inclined persons, is not a matter of people leaving the reincarnation cycle, but of moving to higher vibratory levels while still here.

"Many who are lightworkers … are choosing the tough stuff because we want to get rid of everything that's there. Well, guess what that means? You have to work through it and release it."

Cathy said Bill helped her to work out some past life issues related to her mother. Once, while Cathy was in a light trance, Bill asked Cathy's guide why she had been so reluctant to establish relations with the other side.

"I finally discovered," Cathy said, "that the terror came specifically from one lifetime where I was metaphysically inclined, and I was a healer and doing psychic type things, but I was with a group that was kind of covert. What happened was that someone very close to me betrayed me and turned me in, and I was burned at the stake. I went back to that past life and kind of relived it. It was … the horror of the betrayal, because the person who betrayed me was my sister in that lifetime and my *mother* in this life.

"So there was a lot of stuff to clear there, and it's good that it came up."

Cathy was able to get past old issues with her mother—once they were brought up—with "a lot of forgiveness work and a lot of understanding."

Letting People Know She Was Doing "This Weird Crazy Thing"

After years of meditation Cathy dared to go into a light trance and communicated with higher spiritual realms. Sometimes she would bring their consciousness through by channeling (in other words, allowing them to communicate through her).

"In 1989 this was not all that popular," Cathy recalled. "And I wasn't even going to tell my husband I was doing it. It was like, 'Okay, you guys got me, but I don't have to get out there on the front page of the newspaper.' But as information began to come through that was helpful to Bill, then [to] other people in my life, it was like every place I turned, somebody was in crisis and somebody wanted help … I'm getting pushed to use this for people—and so I did."

Slowly, Cathy began to let a few select people know that she was able to bring guidance through from other realms. She was careful about letting her family know, but she eventually did, with surprising results.

"Basically, Bill was the only one I let know for a very long time, and then my mother came to visit, and I made the terrible mistake of letting her know, and I was thinking, 'Well, I have no idea whether she'll accept this or not but I'm going to do it.' Well, she bought into it instantaneously, and she was my greatest siphon."

With no structure in place, and people anxious to speak with her guides, she found that she was often shoved out of the way, so to speak, and frequently left drained. Eventually, she fell ill.

Cathy's mother lived out of state, and Cathy called her once a week to check on her. Once she had disclosed her ability to give guidance from a trance state, Cathy said her mother was no longer as interested in talking to *her*.

"It got to the point very quickly where she would talk to me for about three minutes and then she would want to talk to my guide … and I let that go on for years before I finally put a stop to it. I said, 'Look, if it isn't good enough for you to talk to your daughter once a week, then we're stopping this.' And that was a huge part of what brought the [illness] on: my mother and my sister. I let them know and they just sucked on to me."

It is not uncommon for intuitives who give out too much to become depleted and then to have health problems.

Learning to Charge Fees and Erect Structure Around Her Work

Slowly, Cathy was coming out of the closet, metaphysically speaking.

She had gotten to the point where she trusted the information that came through her and her role in bringing it through. She let a few friends and family members know about her ability to go into trance and receive information, but she failed to put a structure around it. Consequences followed.

"First, I wouldn't charge for it, and the way that spirit handled that for me was I got used and abused horribly. People would call me; they would keep me on the phone for hours; someone would come over for a reading that I would say I would do for them; I couldn't get them to leave. I was totally drained."

Cathy gave so much to her family and friends that she became ill.

"I developed a condition called Crohn's, which I actually still have," Cathy said. "Crohn's is an intestinal disorder that is like bleeding ulcers but it's deeper ulcers than ulcers of colitis. But I've been very fortunate with it because it flares up infrequently, but it's not gone. It was interesting because before I was actually diagnosed … I remembered driving to work in the mornings hearing myself say, 'They're sucking the life blood out of me.' … So yes, I got ill."

Cathy attributes her physical difficulties to giving too much of herself away.

"Allowing myself, with no boundaries, to just be drained of every bit of life force that could possibly flow through me at the time … It took me years to … realize that spirit was saying, 'Look, you have to get some structure around this.' And finally, somewhere I read, 'The labor is worthy of its hire,' and that kind of thing. So I started charging and then the people in crisis still came, but they didn't come to an unstructured environment."

The first time Cathy charged for a reading was indirectly when ARE, the Cayce organization, paid her to be a staff psychic during a workshop. Cathy auditioned to be on an ARE panel of psychics in the 1980s and was accepted. Cathy said seven psychics auditioned. Of those, two were selected.

"It was exciting," she recalled. "It was kind of a boost … It was a very interesting experience, auditioning, because at that time I was barely doing it professionally. I mean, I was working full time in the corporate world, so I really had very few clients that I was working with."

One of the ARE staff auditioning Cathy sent questions to her, and Cathy went into a trance state and recorded the answers. With the other staff member, a woman, Cathy said it was more like a conversation, similar to the readings she does now.

"They were looking for specific things," she recalled. "I remember her daughter was starting a business, and she wanted to know what looked like a good venue for advertising for her daughter, and I told her it was clear that her daughter needed an ad in the Yellow Pages … (She) asked me, 'How did you get that?' because she was actually getting more into how are you doing this? And I told her, 'Well, I just saw a lot of yellow sheets of paper flying by and it said to me *Yellow Pages*.'

"The thing was, you could either be nervous about doing it or you could just relax and do it. I decided if this is supposed to work and I'm supposed to be a part of their panel, I will be because they called it a panel of professional psychics. If it isn't, it's not the right thing anyway, so don't worry about it. So I was very relaxed going into it."

Emerging from Corporate America, to Daring to Dare

Even after being accepted on a panel of professional psychics, Cathy kept her corporate job for years. Even after being nudged by the other side to give it up.

"It's kind of an interesting story," she said, "because I would say that spirit had to work really hard and move me halfway across the country to make me quit my corporate job. Because I kept getting the message to do it, to do it, and I kept saying, 'I will, I will' ... and obviously I wasn't."

Cathy had a stable job working for a government contractor in Virginia. Then she accepted a promotion that took her and her husband halfway across the country to Colorado. Eighteen months later, another company bought out her firm, and the new company announced that, since they had their own personnel, they would no longer need Cathy's services. She was laid off, she said, quite "unexpectedly and unpreparedly" in 2001.

With time on her hands and financial resources somewhat limited, Cathy began to pursue the intuitive work she'd been doing professionally, and quite covertly, on the side.

"I started doing this full time, and the way I really got into it in terms of building a business was [going to] ... a lot of metaphysical fairs and expos ... I started doing them all to get the exposure," Cathy said. "And that just built. That, plus word of mouth, built my client base. I already had a client base, because I was doing it part-time, [with] clients on the East Coast primarily."

Cathy had gained some of her clients from intuitive training classes she had taken. During class, when it came time for the participants to practice on one another, Cathy was so good at reading her partners that some approached her later for more.

She completed a series of seminars at ARE and eventually studied with author Doreen Virtue, primarily for validation in the way of certification, Cathy said, as she had been studying at home for years.

Still, after moving to Colorado in 2001, she was deep in the closet, metaphysically. While still firmly entrenched in the corporate world, she was extremely reluctant to go public with her rather strange offerings. That changed as her client base built and she had little time to reflect on what she was doing, because more and more of her time was devoted to *doing* it.

The Trance State and How Readings Can Be Useful

Cathy considered what a trance state is like for her. When someone speaks directly to her guides while she is in trance, such as when Bill asked about the tractor, she *is* consciously aware, though somewhat dimly.

"I'm there; I know what's coming through me at the time that it's coming through me. When it's over, it's like having had a dream. If I talk about it to someone immediately, then I'll remember it; on the whole, I won't remember it at all. Just like a dream, it will be gone—except a few experiences that are really outstanding, like viewing a higher dimension or having an incredible symbol come in. Those stayed with me. But for the most part I am not an unconscious channel; I am conscious when I'm channeling. If a fire broke out in the room, I would know it.

"But, yes, it is an altered state of consciousness," she said.

In giving intuitive readings now, Cathy is not in a trance state. She is in conscious communication with her guides and angels and with the guides and angels of the client she is reading for.

Cathy said the overall purpose of giving intuitive readings, for her at least, is "to make people feel empowered, inspired, and to get on with their lives in a powerful way ... To make them all that they can be.

"When I'm doing a reading for someone else, it is always ultimately under the guidance of their guides and angels," she said. "Their guides and angels are going to tell me, is this person ready to hear this? Is it something that should be said now? What's the benefit either way?"

Cathy believes her intuitive readings benefit others by "introducing people to the concept of angels, the concept of guides, the concept that there is something much bigger than the physical, much bigger than time and space ...

"The other thing is, I think when people are ready to open, their souls will also take them to a psychic, guide them, or lead them, or coincidentally bring them into the space of a psychic, so that the soul can start to talk to them."

Using Discernment in What She Shares, and Knowing the Future Has Options

When Cathy is not supposed to share something that she sees during a reading, her guides and her own knowingness let her know it.

"In readings, things will come through *for me,* but I will clearly get that, no, this is not the time [to share that information]. I tune into the guides and angels and the soul of the person that I'm doing the reading for, and you don't actually have to ask them [whether to disclose something]; they will not hesitate to let you know," she said and laughed. "The idea is to be open, to stay open ...

"If you approach someone [with some information] who is not ready, you can do him enormous harm, because if you go there too soon, that person is bound to shut down and shut down with a big heavy iron door slamming shut. You have just delayed that person's progress, and, really, we don't want to be doing that for people. And that's something that people should know, and people that give readings should know, because sometimes you just get so enthusiastic about what you see or what you get that you want to share it all. So, let's have some discernment here."

Most people who work with guidance from higher levels will be advised by their guides to use discernment in what they share, if they will just pay attention. The information she might see, but does not share, varies with the person being read.

"It's individual," Cathy said. "It's not infrequent that people will ask about death and when they are going to die, and, basically, that's not something that's given. Sometimes they [the guides] talk about potential exit points, and most people have five or six of those ... times that they may decide to leave. But ... they're only potential you see.

"One of the things that I always try to make very clear to people is that when you are predicting the future, you are predicting the future based on exactly the way things are *now.* And as people use their free will to make different choices, they set up different futures for themselves, or they can. So predicting the future is never cast in stone. There is nothing that we can't change."

Cathy said this easily explains why good intuitives are often wrong in what they predict: People have the power and the free will to change what may be.

"Sometimes dire predictions will come into play and be shared because the person is also given the tools to change that. 'How can I choose a different path?' 'Well, here are the ways. Here are the things that you can do to change that in your life ...'

"There's no across-the-board list of this is right and this is wrong [to share]. It's one of the things that I like about channeling, because I trust that the angels and the soul of the person that I'm reading for, who are always participating in the reading, know what is for the highest good of that person, in this moment."

Sometimes things are shown to her for *her* own learning. This would be premature for her to share with the client.

"Sometimes they'll show me things and say, 'Don't tell them this now,'" Cathy said. "And the reason that they do that, I think, is for my benefit, because I'm following a time line or I'm looking at something ... that's energetically around the question that the person has asked ...

"Often I will get people who ask, 'Where am I going to move to?' and the answer I will get is, 'This is not for them to know right now,' because they'll move prematurely. You can give someone so much information that they will want so much to jump ahead. And then they will have messed up everything that their soul has set up, and it'll have to start over again. It's like you just threw a monkey wrench into everything."

It is not enough just to be intuitive, it would seem; one must also aspire to be an intuitive who heeds the guidance given them.

Prayer in Her Life and Work

Before she begins any reading, Cathy prays and asks that whatever is for the highest good of the person in the moment to come through. Prayer plays a major role in her life.

"I'd say it's huge," Cathy said, "because, basically, I believe that prayer is something that we do all the time. When we're focusing, where our focus goes, I really believe that *that* is prayer. I used to believe that prayer was talking to God, and meditation was listening to God; now I believe that they really are kind of one and the same. Prayer, when it takes you to a higher dimension of consciousness—and it can—is just as effective as meditation.

"The problem with prayer, as it is practiced culturally in a broad sense—and I don't mean to be judgmental—is that prayer is like supplication. You know, prayer is begging, prayer is asking, prayer is almost like crying out. So prayer doesn't have the sense of personal empowerment that we actually need, the way it's done by very many people."

She alluded to how it is suggested that we pray in the Bible, King James Version, that "whatsoever ye shall ask in prayer, believing, ye shall receive."

"Prayer can be very powerful ... By and large most of mass consciousness get to prayer when we're begging. And that is a totally disempowered place to be."

Cathy suggests that a better alternative would be to set our intention first.

"Now, you've heard the phrase, 'Pray believing,'" Cathy said. "Well, if you pray believing, *then* you are empowered. And that's totally different than the prayer of supplication."

Cathy feels that many people don't know how to pray effectively. She suggested that some churches might have intended to teach people supplication, in part to keep people dependent on the church.

"I never ... do a reading now or did one back then that I didn't start the whole thing by saying to spirit and to God and to the person's soul: 'Show me what is for the highest good for this person at this time.' I always start that way. Because what's the point in me knowing anything else, you know? Certainly I'm not going to tell them anything else, or I don't want to tell them anything else, let's put it that way.

"I start every reading that way. Wouldn't even think of not doing that. It's vitally important."

Using prayer is the only way that she can feel secure in doing her work.

"I mean, probably we [psychics] could go into a trance state and go skating around in all the information that's out there and pick up all kinds of stuff, but suppose it isn't relevant, or suppose it isn't wonderful for them to know at this moment? I don't want to go there. I'm not willing to take that risk. I'm not willing to lay my soul growth on the line."

"I think that it is very important for people that are doing this work and for healers or [people in] any other kind of spiritual work to be responsible. They need to know some of the potential pitfalls, what's out there, that could happen."

Then Cathy returned to a lighter note. "But I so enjoy it," she said. "I mean, it's my passion."

How We May Create What We Believe

We are all intuitive, Cathy believes, and we create our lives through our beliefs.

"Everyone is psychic. It's how much do they pay attention to it, how willing are they to believe it, how open are they to it? Because if they don't believe it, then they're not getting it.

"Belief is the bottom-line factor of what manifests in our lives, always. That's why working on the belief system is so important, if we really want to get good at manifesting what we desire."

What we believe is critical to what we manifest and create in life, she said.

"Most of us don't know what we believe, especially in an area that we seem to be stuck in … and therefore we don't know what's causing us to create the way we are, because beliefs are such an integral part of ourselves. To us it's just the way it is—it's not something we believe, it's fact. Which of course is not true. Beliefs are beliefs. In fact … a belief is just something you've thought about often enough that you've made it true in your life."

People are powerful beings, she said, much more so than most realize.

Intuitives Differ from One Another, as Do Clients

Different psychics work on different levels, with different purposes and intents, Cathy said.

"It depends on the psychic, it depends on what the psychic's mission is," Cathy said. "Not all psychics are focused on the spiritual path and spiritual growth. And to me, that's exactly what … intuitive ability …

is for. But then again, that's *my* mission. And it's not that I judge others, it's just that I know that it's not the same thing [with all psychics]."

At one time in her career, Cathy seemed to have a number of clients who were only calling with questions such as, 'What bar do I go to to meet the next guy?' That type of work was so unfulfilling, Cathy said, that she asked her guides and angels to bar the door, so to speak.

"My work is ... primarily to help people grow spiritually, to open more to their souls, to find their life work, to clear blocks that are in their way. It's not the third dimensional stuff of, 'Where am I going to meet my next mate?' or, you know, that kind of thing. Can I help with that? I can, but I don't enjoy it.

"And so I simply told my gatekeeper guide, 'These are the people that I want you to send someplace else besides me,'" she said and laughed lightly. "There are a lot of psychics around, send them to someone else. These are the ones I want you to bring in.

"And it works!"

In her practice, especially in the early days, another annoyance was clients who wanted to test her.

"The other people I wanted to keep out are the testers," Cathy said. "The people who ... were really interested in proving that it wasn't true. I had a level of annoyance with that because to me it was a total waste of my time."

She has felt that way since she got into the work.

"I've never felt that it was my job to convince anyone that my philosophy is correct or the right way. I've always felt that, basically speaking, spirit is going to bring to you, because of your vibrational frequency, those who are like you. But when you put yourself out in a psychic fair, you *are* really opening some doors. (And I don't do that anymore, by the way.) ... It was a way to start building my clientele and getting my name out there ... But now I know that people who need me will find me. And my work is 99 percent referral."

Recognizing Guides and Angels by Their Vibrations

Cathy spoke some about working with angels, who she feels hail from the realms of divinity.

"Unless we invite them in, we are not fully utilizing that power in our lives," Cathy said. "Inviting your angels in is really critically important because once you invite them in, they bring in synchronicity. They open opportunities for you, new doorways that weren't even there. People that you couldn't possibly meet. A phrase in a song will answer your life's problem for the day.

"And it doesn't have to be anything formal," Cathy emphasized. "When I get up in the morning ... I basically say, 'Come on, guys, let's do this day.' ... But if you don't invite them, they won't, because that law of free will says they can't. And no one in the hierarchy of divinity ever, ever takes a chance on crossing that line of the law of free will."

When she gives readings, angels sometimes come forward and identify themselves. She said some people have two angels, and others have more, depending on what they're working on and what the angels are there to assist with.

"Each angel will identify what he or she is there for, how they most help, and they usually give a name, although angels don't have names," Cathy said. "They only do that for humans. They recognize each other by vibratory rate and color."

Cathy understands this system of identification because it is the one she uses.

"I understand that very well because, in channeling, I know that I recognize all the guides, anyone who comes through me, through vibratory rate and only through that."

It is risky to do otherwise.

"When I sit down, by the time I sit down, I know who's coming through because I have already felt the vibration around me, and that's how I know who it is, by the rate of vibration. Then, when I start to channel, they usually tell the audience who they are, just because people like to know.

"But I will tell you this too, and this is a part of growing and evolving: Every one of them channels through my authentic being, and the authentic being that has come through me is kind of a combination of the higher self, the soul, and the God within. They step down their energy, and they come through the highest part of my being."

Sometimes she acts as a medium, connecting people with those who have crossed over. But again, she is careful.

164

"In terms of connecting people to someone who has crossed over to the other side, my work is *never* allowing a discarnate to enter my body. There is always an intermediary there. I may be talking directly to the soul who has crossed over, but I have my guides. I'm always protected."

Additional Protective Measures

Even early in her work, she took protective measures when she opened herself up to communication with other realms. She doesn't channel as much now because she has direct communication in place at all times. But in the early days she brought sources through from other dimenions of consciousness, and she was very careful.

"In the beginning, I used very powerful protective measures before I would channel, and the most powerful one is the archangel protection," Cathy said. "You call Archangel Raphael to stand on your right side, Archangel Gabriel stands on the left, Archangel Ariel stands behind you, and Archangel Michael stands in front of you. And your instructions to them are that they are to protect you from any negativities and anything untoward that comes in the vicinity of your energy field and then they … form like a cocoon around you so that you are totally protected.

"Many people get into trouble because they have started out [channeling], and they leave themselves wide open, and you leave your solar plexus [chakra or energy center] wide open and you are just basically asking for trouble, because you want everything to go through your heart. The heart has filters … My connection to all my clients is a heart-to-heart connection.

"If you allow people to connect with you through the solar plexus, there are no filters. Whatever is there [when] you're wide open is coming in. Healers get sick. They take on the illness of the people that they're working on, because their solar plexus is open. Psychics get drained because their solar plexus is open."

Cathy protects herself daily. She uses the four archangels' protection technique and puts a white light around herself, with a violet light around that.

"The reason for that is the white light will reflect back any negativity to its source. Well, do we really want to do that? No, we don't. The violet light absorbs the negativity and transmutes it into neutral energy… so I am not perpetuating negative energy out there by just reflecting it back."

Energy is thought to be neutral until we "qualify" it with our thoughts, feelings, actions, or the like. Using the violet transmuting flame or violet light restores the energy to a positive or an unqualified state.

From Seeing Malevolent Entities to Considering Exorcism

Once, Cathy saw something very evil in someone's energy field, but what stood out for her more than that was how totally protected she felt, thanks to the angels and guides she works with.

"I did a reading once, very early on … and when she [the client] sat down in front of me, there was the most malevolent entity attached to her energy field," Cathy recalled. "I felt totally and completely protected. And it was very clear to that entity that he could not affect me and that my job was not to force him out from her, because she was not ready to let him go. She had made some kind of an agreement with him, but I *was* going to tell her about him. So that was a very interesting experience.

"Given the level of fear that I have had in the past, that was so interesting to me to feel so totally protected in that situation. Because that was far and away the ugliest energy I have ever touched."

She did disclose the presence to the client because it was adversely affecting the woman's health and life. The woman took the news well because she knew it subconsciously.

"At the same time, she [the client] couldn't break the connection that she had made and when she left me, she was not ready to do it still, but she had a clear understanding of why she had all this trauma going on in her life. And she was open to accepting it, the information, at least."

Cathy has seen entities attached to clients at other times, and she leaves it to the guides and angels of the person to advise her as to whether or not to share this information.

"When I'm doing a reading for someone else, it is always ultimately under the guidance of their guides and angels," Cathy said. "Their guides and angels are going to tell me, is this person ready to hear this? Is it something that should be said now? What's the benefit either way?"

However, when it comes to what she calls true possession—when an evil entity has full control of a person—Cathy believes a professional should be called in.

"You need, not necessarily a Catholic priest, because it doesn't have to be *their* exorcism, but you need to have someone who knows what they're doing and who is so totally confident in what they're doing that they will not be intimidated by anything this entity does through this person's physical body. Besides, you are taking a risk of hurting the person's physical being if you don't know what you're doing."

"There's a movie out called *The Exorcism of Emily Rose*. I recommend that people interested in this go and see that movie, because it can be that difficult."

Cathy would not perform an exorcism.

"Even if I felt that I knew what to do, I wouldn't do it, because I'm not willing to take that risk," Cathy said. "And that's a choice on my part."

Cathy distinguished between attachment and possession.

"An attachment, you're having your life force drained off, and you're having experiences that are not very pleasant. You can have health issues. But possession, that entity totally takes over. At least at periods of time.

Cathy said before she takes any kind of action she prays that whatever is for the highest good of the client be served, because it's possible that prior to the life the client agreed for a given situation to occur in his or her life

Not Judging Others or Oneself

Cathy doesn't know of anyone who doesn't struggle with judging others, including herself.

"It's easy to have problems with judging people, because all you have to do is get in your mind instead of your heart, let your ego have any kind of play, because the ego is the quintessential judger, you know?" Cathy said. "And the thing that I find that I have to be most careful about is looking at someone and feeling sorry for them. Because as soon as you do that, you are pouring negative energy into them; you are feeding the energy of the space that they are in, the feelings that they are feeling."

Since we are highly creative beings, we must be careful to focus on the positive, lest we lend power to the negative by our attention to it.

"You want ... *always* to see a person at the soul level and see their potential power," Cathy said.

Although energy is basically neutral, the universe endeavors to oblige us by giving us what we expect. She said if we expect hardships or the like, hardships we will get. In other words, there *is* power in positive thinking.

As for judging, Cathy's higher guidance once indicated to her that it is not so much that we *shouldn't* judge others, but that we *cannot*, because we do not have enough information.

"This didn't come from me. This came through a channeled reading that I did ... that said, 'How can you judge when you cannot have a broad enough perspective? You can't see everything in this person's lifetime. You can't see all the past lives. You can't [see] what's there in the future, and you can't see what that person's soul is working out at the moment. So how can you know? And how do you know that this person that you think is doing something awful ... is not truly playing a very important role in the life play of the person that he or she is angry with? How do you know that that's not the exact situation this person needs at this moment, and its soul has gone to a great deal of effort to set it up? You just do not know.'"

Judgment gets in the way of a pure flow of higher consciousness because we taint it with our judgment, and it isn't pure anymore. She said the information she brings through is clearer if she is open and avoids judging.

"I would add this," Cathy said. "Self judgment is ... absolutely the most destructive thing that we do. And we are actually no better, no more skilled, no more capable at self-judgment than we are at judgment of others. Because we can't see the whole picture for ourselves either. Do we know all of our past lives? Do we know everything that has

influenced us and brought us to where we are? Do we know w
every line of our soul contract? No. So we might as well give it
useless. It's a waste of time, and it's almost always negative."

Receiving Feedback about Her Work

Intuitives often don't get the benefit of feedback from clients, which
Cathy feels is unfortunate. However, one reading turned into a precious
memory for Cathy.

"One of the most rewarding things was, I had a woman come to
me at the third or fourth conference I did down at Virginia Beach.
She couldn't sleep at night; she ground her teeth all the time," Cathy
recalled. "She was just totally torn up. And I did a reading for her.

"It was very clear that the reason that she was totally torn up was
that, when she was eighteen years old, she had an abortion, and she had
never been able to accept that. We talked about that, and in the course
of the reading she discovered that the baby, this soul that she aborted at
that time, was actually her three-year-old daughter now. So there was
no point in her being concerned.

"And it so changed her life. They had an ending [event] at the
conference, and this woman's sister came up to me, and she said, 'I
don't know what you told my sister in her reading … but I know that
you have changed her life. Because the night after the reading she slept
through the night. She does not grind her teeth anymore …'

"That to me was one of the most rewarding experiences I had had … I
will never forget how that felt. I told the sister the same thing I tell everyone:
It is not me. It comes through me, but it's not me."

Now that she has an established business, Cathy also has the benefit
of seeing her clients grow and benefit from their sessions. But in the
early days of conferences and the like, often it was just Bill who really
appreciated her efforts.

"I'm working for years and not getting any validation except for
my husband basically. Or through things like the tractor, or what to
do about the apple tree that has something wrong with it, that kind of
thing. That was some validation because it actually worked."

Cathy referred to an incident when their apple tree was ailing. Bill
asked Cathy's guides what to do, and the remedy worked.

Frequently clients don't realize the value of what comes through in a reading, until later.

"One of the reasons I've insisted on taping every conversation … is because … if they listen to the tape three months later or a year later, they will hear something on it they didn't hear the first time. Because, when you're giving your angels and your guides a chance to talk to you, boy, they jump in with both feet, and they give you everything they can in the allotted period of time."

She laughed delightedly.

Differing Intuitive Abilities

"It comes out in a lot of readings that people who are in this work … are just basically getting drained out," Cathy said. "See, people have different kinds of psychic abilities. There's claircognizance, which is clear knowing; clairaudience [which is] clear hearing; clairvoyance [which is] clear seeing, but clairsentience is the toughest one. Clairsentience is clear feeling, and most clairsentients, if they don't know to protect their solar plexus, are getting beaten up all the time … They're the ones whose bodies take on all the negative stuff.

"And the way to protect your solar plexus is to ask your angels to put a metal plate … over the solar plexus, front and back, and seal the edges. Those who are primarily clairsentient need to do that every morning and every time they go into any place where there will either be negative energy or too much energy, like a mall, a party, a theater. Because clairsentients, that's just their nature, to pick up everybody else's feelings. *Imagine* that!"

As for Cathy, she considers herself primarily clairvoyant. She has stunningly clear visions, which she narrates in her readings. She said that the ability to *see* is something she worked to achieve.

"My dominant psychic ability was claircognizance, which is a clear knowing," Cathy said. "The information was coming through the claircognizance, but you're just not satisfied. That's the toughest one to realize that you're actually using intuitive ability, because you just think everybody knows these things."

Despite being intuitive and *knowing* things, she always wanted to be able to "see." She had a few experiences with hearing clairaudiently, but clairvoyance or having pictures come into her mind's eye was what she longed for. For a while, she tried too hard. Once she got out of her own way, it came easily.

"Obviously, since it's now my dominant way [of getting information] and it's so easy for me, it must have been the way that I've done it in past lifetimes. I worked at it for quite a while and I couldn't get it, just couldn't get visualization. And when I stopped trying, it started happening …

"And it came very subtly, because I didn't even realize that I was seeing things. I was doing readings, and all of a sudden it dawned on me, 'Wait a minute, I'm seeing things while I'm hearing this.' Mostly, anyone will find, when you try too hard, you block yourself, because you become too wrapped around wanting it to happen and you never relax and allow it to happen. It's very important, because relaxing and surrendering are the answers 99 percent of the time. Whenever you're trying hard, your mind is involved … and whenever the mental is involved, you are at best slowing yourself down, and at worst you're blocking it."

Relaxing into Meditation

Cathy uses the breath to relax for meditation.

"If you breathe deeply through your nose and out through your mouth and you do it long enough, your body will start to relax no matter what; it simply happens," Cathy said. "So, what I do … I just move into the stillness because … I have a habit pattern of that now, and I understand it … Now I don't have to be in a meditative state for guidance to come through me. It happens when I'm driving. It happens when I'm walking around. You know, I don't specifically have to meditate to do that."

While advancing along the path of spiritual growth and development, it is important to discover and experience our "observer" self—that part of ourselves that is always watching and which is actually our higher self, our soul, or the God within. It is what Cathy refers to when she mentions our "authentic" self.

"When we are attuned to that self, it's like we're functioning on two levels," Cathy said. "We're doing our thing, but we have an awareness at a deeper level of what that thing is that we're doing and how we're doing it."

Cathy said if you were to explain this to young children, they would probably say that they do it. She said various states of consciousness can actually be scientifically measured in terms of brain waves.

"Young children and animals tend to live at the alpha level of consciousness [of] the brain wave measurements ... for a certain number of years. Animals are always there. It's when we get into the beta level that we start to get messed up," she said and laughed gently.

"One of the reasons for meditation is to move into the alpha. And some people actually go lower; they go into theta and delta. The yogis who get down to delta are the ones who can stop their hearts and lie on a bed of nails and all those phenomenal things, because that's how much control they have, and that's a very very slow frequency of brain waves.

"Beta is the fastest [frequency of brain wave]," Cathy said, "but it registers the lowest in terms of consciousness."

Cathy has much to say on the importance of getting the chatty mind out of the way, if we are to access higher levels of consciousness. She trained for it.

"Have you ever heard of Silva Mind Control?" Cathy asked. "That's all done at the alpha level. You teach yourself how to go into the alpha state of consciousness, and you work from there in a very conscious way ... I trained in it. It was fascinating."

Cathy found Silva Mind Control methods very helpful. Anything that teaches you to experience that level of consciousness and to function there for any period of time, she said, is helpful in preparing yourself to access, experience, and sustain higher levels of consciousness.

Interpreting the Symbols She Sees

When doing readings, Cathy is highly visual. She generally starts each session with a narrative of a scene unfolding before her mind's eye. Earlier in her work, she tried very hard to decode things she saw that were symbolic.

"For the most part, there's no dictionary. You know, it just depends, because it's different for everyone," Cathy explained. "And one of the interesting things … that makes it very clear is, strawberries as a symbol will mean something very different for someone that loves them, and someone that breaks out in hives when he eats them."

For a long time Cathy worked earnestly to interpret what she saw. Sometimes, when she couldn't get clarity, she put the symbol to the client to consider. A time came, however, when Cathy no longer had to work to figure out what something meant.

"When I first started doing readings … I got a lot of symbols because I'm very visual," Cathy related. "I would try and try to figure out what they meant, and I would usually get there, but then one time … I had this symbol, I don't remember what it was, but it was like [I was asking], 'What is it?' … And they told me. And it hit me immediately."

She suddenly realized that she could simply ask the guides and angels what the symbols meant. She asked them if this was correct, and they assured her it was. She said, previously, they wouldn't interfere with her free will, all the while she was choosing to struggle.

"If I wanted to try to figure it out, they were going to let me do that forever," Cathy said, sighing at the thought of it. "So I never fail to ask anymore. It's so much easier."

Cathy emphasized yet again how those from the ranks of divinity will not interfere with humans' free will. We must ask for their assistance.

The Guides Who Guide Her

Cathy believes that her guides are from the ranks of the hierarchy of divinity. They are from a group called the Ascended Masters, who are said to be the guardians of humanity, as assigned with that duty by still higher levels.

The Great White Brotherhood of Ascended Masters is said to include high spiritual beings known from humanity's history, such as Jesus, Buddha, and the like. This group has been known in some esoteric circles for centuries, and they are said to hail from the upper vibratory levels of the spirit world.

Early in her work, Cathy knew her guides by names. She thinks this was to facilitate an ease in her sense of working with them. Some of those she was in contact with are known to humans as historical figures: St. Paul, St. Francis of Assisi, and Jesus, for instance. Whereas the Ascended Masters used names for identity purposes in the past, Cathy has now been guided to recognize them by their vibrations or auric colors instead. Perhaps this is to avoid the potential pitfall of engaging an entity claiming to be someone it is not.

Cathy speaks of the masters in reverent yet familiar terms.

The Human Lifestream and Evolution

Cathy counts herself among those she calls "star-seeded lightworkers." She said they have not been on the entire journey of development with the life stream known as humanity, but came later, to help.

"In order to really be of help, we had to experience everything that all the souls have, which means we had to get down, we had to have the tough lives, we had to have the closed-off-from-spirit lives and all of that stuff," Cathy said.

The so-called star-seeded lightworkers came from other energy systems, other planets, other galaxies, and the like, Cathy explained.

Cathy sees a time in the not too distant future when all of mankind will take an evolutionary leap to a higher level of consciousness. She believes those higher realms are already becoming accessible to mankind.

But in the meantime, humanity has to expose and clean up some of the darker, hidden parts of itself, which can be witnessed in conflicts in the Middle East, corporate scandals, and the like. Toxins, so to speak, have to be discharged and released. Cathy considers this as being darkest just before the dawn, for she does see the dawning of a golden age on the horizon for humankind—a time when love rules and guides the way.

Cathy believes that extraterrestrials (ETs) are part of the picture, in several respects.

"There are so many extraterrestrials who are here, and they are hanging out here all the time in motherships and whatever, basically waiting for us to be ready to allow them to make an appearance without us freaking out," Cathy said. "All of the ETs who are in our vicinity and who are working with us are under the direction of the Ascended

Masters, at this point. The Ascended Masters are the guardians of this planet ... and their greatest mandate is, 'Do no harm; you will not bring fear.' And so they're holding off, I mean, they're working through a lot of lightworkers ... but they're not appearing on the White House lawn."

Cathy is cheered when she says ETs could help humanity make the planet pristine again.

"But again, the universal law of free will reigns supreme," Cathy said. "And so they can't interfere. They have to be invited. They even have to be invited to work with individuals. I mean, they'll make some contact, they'll kind of knock on the door, and if the door is opened, then fine, they'll work with individuals."

One reason extraterrestrials have such an interest in humankind at this stage of our development is because we can choose to develop from the heart, rather than develop more of the mental side.

"There are many highly evolved ETs who are very interested in watching us evolve through the heart, because they didn't," Cathy explained. "They evolved through their minds. So we're the first ones to do it through the heart. Remember Spock on *Star Trek*? Not a very emotional being. He would be one who evolved through his mind, not through his heart. See what I'm saying? That sets kind of an example."

Legions may be gathering to see if we humans can pull off being heart centered for our next leap of evolution. Some say difficulties may be wrought as old systems crumble, but that humankind *will* rise, out of a chrysalis, like a butterfly, into a new age of caring and connection with each other and with the higher realms. Cathy leaves with the thought that legions of ETs are in the ethers around earth, watching to see if humanity can achieve this new age.

Mary Roach

God Speaks to the Sons and Daughters of Men

Mary Roach has a lively presence, which is sometimes punctuated by a rapid-fire, seemingly tireless manner of speaking. Her hair is alight with blonde streaks, and her small nose is upturned. She is down to earth and candid, with an abiding, if somewhat understated, sense of humor.

Though only in her mid-forties, Mary is a somewhat celebrated psychic. Her husband, Kevin Todechi, is a prolific writer and currently the Executive Director of the Association for Research and Enlightenment (ARE), an organization based on the teachings of the renowned psychic Edgar Cayce, who died in 1945. Cayce left tomes of inspired writings. But even before Mary's union with Kevin, she was one of the most highly regarded and sought-out psychics associated with ARE.

Mary's husband tells this story. Years ago, he went to see Mary for an intuitive reading. Since they both lived in Virginia Beach, Virginia, he was able to go in person. He was newly divorced. Toward the end of his reading, Mary announced, "You have a new relationship coming up."

"Oh, no," he interjected, "I'm just getting over a divorce, and I am *not* getting into a new relationship. I'm through with that for a while."

Mary shrugged, and said, "I don't think so. She's here." And then she added, "And this one's going to give you a run for your money."

What neither of them knew was that the relationship Mary spoke of would be with her. Casual observation suggests that she *does* give him a run for his money.

Mary Roach is a busy person. She has a full-time intuitive practice, teaches intuitive training classes, works out at a gym for strength training, and helps to raise their small son. Still, when she gives intuitive readings, she is known to give her all, in exhaustive, heartfelt sessions in which she talks at length with a marked rapidity. She makes appointments only twice a year, in January and July, and is quickly booked.

Mary believes an intuitive is best at what interests her most, whether it be health, business, or whatever, and she says *her* abiding interest is life purpose and/or life lessons. She requests that clients send questions prior to their appointments, and she encourages them to inquire about life purpose and/or life lessons. She also asks that they send a photo of themselves, for two reasons: for the permission to tune into their energy, as conveyed by the loan of the object; and to sense their vibration, realized through the eyes.

It is Mary's belief that a client participates in his or her reading to some extent by their intention. She said when she reads for someone who isn't really sure why he or she is getting the reading, it often isn't a good reading. It's too nebulous, for the client has not set their intention to *know.*

Before she gives a reading, Mary sets *her* intention. In her intuitive training classes, she advises students that *their* intention dictates the clarity of the information received—and the source of it.

"Your intention says, 'I intend consciously to tune into God for an answer,'" Mary said. "That's where you want to go for an answer. It cleans up the language and the garbage."

Mary prays before each reading. She said, as Cayce found decades ago, God the Father speaks directly to the sons and daughters of men, even as He has promised.

Was She a Psychic as a Child?

Mary claims she didn't have any natural psychic ability as a child. She uses that seeming lack of ability now as a springboard in her classes to lead people to the belief that *they* can do what she does. One thing about her background, however, is curious: As a child, she could not look most people in the eye. Since she uses this technique now in her work, to see into the soul or the vibration of the client, one wonders if this might have been too much for her as a child.

Mary cannot say with certainty if any genetic traces of her intuitiveness can be tracked to her parents, for she was adopted. Her interest in metaphysics, however, has existed for as long as she can remember.

"I've been interested in metaphysical phenomena all through my life," she said. "I used to do telepathic exercises with my friend when I was in seventh grade, to see if we could get anything right. We certainly liked it, but if you went to the library, all you could get were books on witches and stuff ... and that wasn't really what I was looking for. I was more interested in metaphysical type things, but there wasn't a lot at the time."

Mary grew up mostly in Massachusetts, with a brief but beneficial sojourn in Hawaii.

"I was adopted, so I had a family that was a little bit older than some of the other parents, which ... I'm really grateful for, actually. They were very responsible, very good parents. We just had a small family: my sister, myself, and my mom and dad—and dogs ... We started off in Massachusetts and then moved to ... Hawaii. And I will say that moving to Hawaii was actually probably a very spiritual experience for me, because I was a very anxious kid."

Mary went to parochial school and she had to be bused, which was difficult for her.

"It was in the sixties and it was just very stressful for me. Just the idea of just getting out there," she said, laughing, "was just a big stressful experience, and I know that I was given some kind of nerve medicine. I have no idea what it was to this day; it could've been Robitussin ... But I was a very nervous kid, very anxious, very afraid of my own shadow ... It was a good thing I was sheltered in some ways in those early years, because I probably couldn't have handled any more than I got."

Hawaii, however, held a promise that it kept.

"When we moved to Hawaii, I felt completely comfortable there. I felt completely at home. You know, the beauty, the fragrance, the flowers, the rainbows, the clouds. It was such an extraordinarily beautiful place. First of all, it's very calming when you see beauty all the time ... [I was] impacted in a very positive way by the nature of this place."

Mary also feels that having a positive religious influence in her life helped spiritually, as did the religious diversity of those on the island.

"I was raised Catholic ... and actually, that church was a particularly good one. It was called, I think, Holy Trinity, and it had a really great ... education program for kids. You had to go get this education in order to get your first communion, your first confession, and all that stuff, and it was a very good program. So that was the way spirituality made sense to me. I still have the books, believe it or not, because they were really, really well done.

"You'd walk into a person's house, you'd take off your shoes when you went in the door most often, and ... they might have a Buddha on the television because they were from another country ... That was where I really learned a lot about things, was Hawaii."

Her idyllic time in Hawaii would not last, but it did help to prepare her for the world.

"We moved back to Virginia, which was outside of [Washington] D.C.," Mary recalled. "That's a whole different animal. That's a very fast-paced environment and that was different, but ... I was glad we were in Hawaii, because that was a place where you could really relax and see the world differently."

Mary was a highly sensitive child.

"I was probably hypersensitive," she said. "I also couldn't look at people in the eye. And I kind of hid behind my mom ... My mom put up with a lot of stuff from me because I would come home and I would process verbally; I'd just talk to her about everything that ever happened. I could've been home schooled very easily and very happily, but they didn't really have that back then. Interestingly enough, it was good that I wasn't, because I learned to become more social."

Since Mary often speaks in front of groups now, she values that socialization.

Although she doesn't have a sense of having been psychic as a child, Mary admits to a certain psychic sensitivity, though she qualifies it.

"I probably had some psychic information coming through, but I never saw a dead person. I didn't see ghosts. I didn't see angels. At that time, I hadn't seen anything. I was being raised Catholic, so whatever their belief, I was buying it too, and being part of [it] ...

"I did have a strong sensitivity and compassion for other people. I think I had a tremendously strong empathy ... but I didn't have any psychic phenomena-type things happen. You know, no dead guys coming and talking to me, no ghosts showing up, no angels necessarily, until I was older. Then I saw an angel, but before that I never had."

If she was psychic at all, it was in how she perceived others. She maintains her assertion that we can all cultivate psychic abilities, though she thinks it is perhaps easier for those who are especially creative.

"It's something that I think everyone can develop ... After college, that's when I was really able to develop it. It took years to develop; it didn't develop overnight. I was able to do it off the bat and get some things right, but to develop it also means developing a style of how you're going to work with people, developing your own interests, to find out what you're good at [in] working with people, where you might be weaker working with people, you know, that kind of thing."

In addition to the importance of developing an individual style of working, Mary said you have to be willing to put the information out there with the right intention, and then to accept that you have done your best.

"If you always want feedback, you may not always get feedback [from clients]. So you have to do the reading and know in your own consciousness that you did what you should do. Do the right thing, and then you're done."

Early Influences and Development

Mary is eager to acknowledge her mentors. One of the most important influences was a woman she took classes from after she graduated from college.

"I took a class at Cape Cod Community College. It was with a teacher named Pat McKenna, and she was a full-time psychic ... She taught a class on parapsychology, and it was a summer class, and the class would get full. There were people from all walks of life, all ages: sixties, twenties, thirties. I was in my twenties at the time. People just flocked to her. She was actually a really great teacher, and she would have huge classes for her initial class, and then she would ask if ... anybody wanted to continue ... with her in smaller groups."

Those classes helped Mary to develop her psychic abilities. She also credits another early influence with helping her to use her high sensitivity to her advantage.

"The way I teach psychic work is ... from a point of view of sensitivity," Mary said. "The more sensitive the person is, the more they can tune into this; the easier it is for them to tune into this because the more sensitive they are to emotion. So the more emotional a person is, or if they're hypersensitive ... they're going to be able to do this.

"There was a psychic in California. In 1984 I bought her book at a bookstore in Boston. Her name was Marcy Calhoun. She's still around. I recommend her book every time I do a seminar ... the book is called *Are You Really Too Sensitive: How to Develop and Understand Your Sensitivity as the Strength It Is?*"

Mary also studied astrology for a while and has a high regard for it. Astrology readings helped her at a time when she needed them.

"I was an astrology student for a very short time with a very good astrologer named Betty Caulfield, who is in Florida now ... still working. And she did a great reading for me, so I was a real fan ... I would've been interested in being an astrologer. Actually, to this day, a lot of those readings were very accurate back in the eighties, back when I really needed readings.

"I don't think I've known a bad astrologer. I think it's a karmic thing. I also think it's a talent from a past life, and, also, I think they're using a lot of intuition, but they use the [astrology] chart as their field ...

"I always tell people I was never smart enough to be an astrologer, so I had to do psychic work. I was taking classes, and one of the teachers said, 'If you guys are not going to study, it's a waste of your time.' They would be putting up charts and say all [are] anorexic or people who were murdered and you were supposed to figure out what [the commonality] was ... I was too lazy to continue."

Interestingly, Mary began giving impromptu readings to friends, somewhat as a playful thing. She was around a lot of creative people, and they had openness about it.

"New England is actually pretty open to metaphysical phenomena," Mary said. "I knew people who did this stuff, so it wasn't that weird ... Because I was doing a lot of theater, I was around a lot of people who were creative and interesting anyway, so they were people who weren't necessarily as judgmental as mainstream society would be."

Her mentor Pat McKenna helped her yet again, to find the process that worked best for Mary, as a budding psychic.

"It's easier for me to do readings ... straight out ... Once I figured out how my style worked, it was just easier to stick with what I learned. And actually, it was Pat McKenna who helped with style, because in one of our classes we had to do a reading using psychometry, using the technique of holding on to jewelry or car keys or something like that ... Once I learned her technique, it was too hard to go back and do any other technique."

Mary still uses psychometry, which is holding on to something that belongs to the person in order to tune into them. However, Mary thinks it may be a different process than is commonly understood.

"People will say there's a lot of vibration on jewelry or on watches and I'll say there's some, but what it really is—and I realized this over years—you're getting permission from the person's soul to tune into them. When they hand you that jewelry or key or pen that they use all the time, they're giving you permission to tune into them in a more intimate manner, and once you have that permission, you're allowed to do it. That's what I think it really is."

Psychic Training Wheels

Performing was one of her interests. So Mary first practiced on her theater friends.

"I did readings for people in theater ... We'd be sitting after rehearsal or something, and they'd say, 'Well, the thing is, if I get this part,' or 'I'm having a problem with my family,' or 'I need to get a job,' and we would do it [a reading].

"It was Cape Cod; it was the eighties. I never had a negative response from anybody about doing readings. When I moved to Virginia Beach,

I had some negative responses from people who found out that I did readings, some judgmental stuff. I don't tell anybody *now* down here; I don't mention it ..."

Since Mary was mostly playing around with friends, it was a good way to ease into the work.

"There was no pressure, there was no anxiety or anything; I was just helping somebody out ... And I really do feel like the need of the person has a lot to do with the reading ... If they're just somebody coming to my office and they really don't want to be there and they've been dragged by their girlfriend, that's not a reading that's going to go that well. It could, but you don't want to bet on that one going that well ... if they don't want to be there, that's part of the problem. The *need* of the person to get the reading, the stronger the need, I think, the more accurate the reading."

The needs of those she worked with in theater, coupled with their openness, helped Mary to hone her skills.

"I think it started off, sort of designed for success, because the people I worked with ... were very open to it. Some had some problems they wanted to talk about ...

"I started doing readings for money back in '87 ... before that, I don't think I was paid, it was more goofing around. Plus, theater people, they're always broke."

Her friends' openness to metaphysical matters helped lead Mary to other interesting experiences.

"We would go to listen to a medium on stage or go to metaphysical bookstores, so I hung around people who were interested in this. I was always around people that were opened to it. I was taking classes ... I ended up doing more and more of the readings over time. It just grew over time."

Mary's family didn't object to her interests, but neither did they sign up for a session.

"I think my dad thought it was something I was interested in, but it would somehow pass," Mary recalled. "And my mom, my mom's not against it. Nobody's against it. It's like, 'Oh Mary, she does readings or whatever.' They're not impressed overly either!" she said, laughing. "Nobody asks for a reading, generally speaking. I think I've had one aunt who asked for a reading and that's about it."

She reiterated what others in this work have said: No one is a prophet in her own hometown.

"Most psychics don't have family that's necessarily into this stuff," Mary said. "We're just sort of the lone ranger ..."

Because of the nature of her work, she said it's largely a solitary endeavor.

"We work as loners. Healers also work as loners. We work very independently."

By and large, most of the better practicing psychics never set out to be psychics.

"I'd say 90 percent of us get pulled into it," she said. "We don't go to it. It comes to us over time."

Originally, Mary intended to give readings part-time, as a hobby. She was headed for a degree in counseling. At least, she thought that was the plan.

"I would have gone and got a counseling degree in general and gone in that direction, but I just never got around to it, because I ... kept working and doing readings and stuff ... I was never planning on doing this for a living. It's too hard to explain [for one thing]. If you're talking to a person on an airplane for three hours across the country, you don't want to explain it, because they're going to hate it, or they're going to really love it. Either way, there are disadvantages on both sides, so it's just something you don't plan to do."

She thinks anyone who sets out to be a professional psychic is a rare bird, and not likely to get there.

"It would be an unusual person. Anybody who'd want to do it probably isn't going to do it."

ARE Enters Her Life and Launches Her

After college, Mary visited Virginia Beach with a group. She discovered a foundation there related to the work of Edgar Cayce. She was intrigued, especially after she discovered that ARE had a university that offered a graduate-level degree in transpersonal studies.

"We came down to Virginia Beach ..." Mary recalled, "and I heard that there was this place called ARE and I thought, wow, that's an interesting place. I'd heard of Edgar Cayce. I joined the organization ... and I went to be a student at Atlantic University after graduation."

She wanted to work in counseling, which she had done in Massachusetts. Her destiny may have been otherwise however, because, although she applied for dozens of jobs in her field, all her efforts were to no avail.

"I moved here in 1992, and I looked for a job. I applied for, like, fifty-one jobs. I think I interviewed for fourteen. I didn't get any of them. Do you know what I'm saying? ... I had these great conversations with people, and they said, 'Boy we just love your ideas. If you would just get a master's degree, we could hire you,' or 'If you would just have worked for the state, we could hire you,' or 'If you had this kind of degree, we could put you in there ...'

"I had some great interviews where I felt very positive, but in the end they would say, 'We can't hire you because we need to hire a state person' or that kind of thing. So I ended up, really, working full-time for readings from there on out, because I never was short on readings. I was getting the phone calls for the readings and more opportunities for the readings, and people who seemed to like me would tell their friends, 'Oh, you need to get a reading.' So it just seemed like, if I got one person, I got five."

Looking back, Mary believes she wasn't supposed to get another job in human services, that she was intended to do the work she now does.

"The way I figure it is, it's a calling, and either you do it or you don't. If I tried to make it happen, it wasn't going to happen. If I had planned, it wasn't going to happen that way ... I don't think you can plan to do this kind of work."

Almost inadvertently, ARE boosted Mary's credibility in the early years by bringing her on a panel of psychics they convened for a conference held in the early nineties.

"This was the very first conference they had ... [on psychic development]," Mary recalled. "They [had] started running into so many bogus psychics or people who said, 'Hi, I'm in touch with Edgar Cayce and he says this and that' ... so they were really not hosting stuff on psychic development. It was more spiritual development, ancient mysteries. But they decided ... that they could bring psychics in, and they brought nine psychics in, I believe … They did that first conference, and I was a student at Atlantic University …"

Mary had taken a leave of absence from her job at a group home in Massachusetts. If she could find a job in social work in Virginia, she thought it would be her ticket to relocating. She had decided that she wanted—and needed—a degree in transpersonal studies, and ARE was the place to get it.

"I had done readings, and I really wanted to get this degree because I wanted to be able to work with the kind of intensity that I was having with people who were coming in, because some things were very intense. A lot of people who had been molested and been through very traumatic divorces and all kinds of very serious situations, and I just thought the transpersonal degree would help me manage that better.

"The psychic conference they [ARE] hosted was so popular, they ended up being short a psychic, and I actually was asked to test, to see if I was any good, to see if I could do it on the program."

Mary gave readings to two ARE employees, both of whom passed her.

"They said, 'Okay you can be the tenth psychic. If there's any more people in the group we have, you'll take on the extra people.'"

Mary was called on during the conference to give readings to ten people. Afterward, ARE had participants complete questionnaires rating the readings they received.

"They evaluated psychics, and I believe I got a pretty high evaluation … I think I was the first or the second … A friend of mine I ended up doing readings with was right neck and neck with me: Linda Schiller-Hanna. She and I teach a psychic development program [now]; we teach on the road together.

"We didn't know each other [then], we just happened to do really well at the time. The next year we were both invited to come back to the conference, and they started creating a new panel of psychics, because they went by the numbers and the evaluations, and we were both invited to come back."

Mary's requests for readings increased after that exposure.

"Once I got invited back, I just kept getting more and more readings. I had to go home [to Massachusetts] at the end of that semester in May. I had to go back to work, actually, but I ended up getting readings all through … and before I left. I just kept doing reading after reading after reading … I did go back to my job [in Massachusetts] for a time … but that was the beginning of the end right there … because I left in June of '92."

A full-time job as a psychic and intuitive had come to Mary.

"I got so many readings at the next conference that, if I wanted to make a go of it, I could've, because ARE attracts people from all over the country, and there are readings from all over the country … So I had a lot of people who … would come into town, a lot of people with serious things that I'd never worked with before, like kids who had died in car accidents and stuff, so I just was exposed to a broader range of experiences. It was really interesting."

Once Mary was on ARE's list of likely psychics, they told her that she would need to develop a technique with which she could read clients at a distance.

"ARE—years ago when they first did that conference in 1992—they basically said, 'Well those of you who are going to do readings with our program are going to have to be able to do readings at a distance, and do you have a technique?' At the time I hadn't even thought of it; I always thought I'd do them in person. I realized that I had to come up with something real quick.

"I knew I could read photographs, so I told the people I could read a photograph of a person and … when they send that photograph, that's like giving permission."

With her long distance technique established, Mary was on her way as a professional. She still gets a little peeved when people won't send a photo.

"A lot of time people won't send a picture of themselves. What I'm really looking for is not what they look like, because I never remember that kind of stuff; what I really care about is what the vibration is through the eyes. *That's* the distance technique."

If clients fail to send a photo, Mary still has their written questions, which gives her something tangible.

The work as a professional psychic can be tiring at times. Although the money's good, it isn't great unless you charge a massive hourly fee or write books that are successful. Still, there are payoffs, she said, sweet rewards that make the work well worthwhile.

Sweet Rewards of the Work

Mary talked about some of the best things about doing readings.

"When I've been *right*, that's been the nicest thing, when I've felt like I was really nailing something," she said. "There's a flow to it that's … a very positive feeling. When you're in the flow … it's almost like it is sort of a perfect harmonious experience in that place."

The flow, however, isn't always easy to attain.

"Sometimes it's hard to get to that place, and some situations are more challenging, since you're working with the public. And so, you get all kinds of people with all kinds of issues and, some people, you're going to have trouble getting into that flow with them."

She likes working for herself and, if you will, for God.

"Working for yourself, you don't really answer to anybody but God. And the other thing I've found is, over the years God is more in control of your schedule. So I would have times when, say, a whole day would cancel out, and I would look at the date in the book and say, 'What is going on, why did everybody cancel out?' And then something would happen, and I'd end up not being able to work that day anyway. Sometimes the synchronicity that you get to witness—you know?"

Mary appreciates the spiritual aspect of her work.

"Some of the other good stuff is talking about spirituality and God all the time, and then, sometimes, people actually end up feeling pretty good about it. Somebody'll say, 'Boy that was really great,' or 'That was the highlight of my year' … Sometimes you get really positive feedback …

"I can't personally take credit for it, but it certainly feels good that I was there … It was me being open at the time … giving the right information … It's not my personality doing the reading, it's something else. My personality has to move out of the way to a certain degree …

"So when it really works well like that, and it does really help people, I like hearing that feedback. That part's nice … If I did get out of the way and I did interpret everything properly, that is good."

Mary especially enjoys what she learns.

"Finding out what the souls are really about," she said. "Looking at the interaction of how the karmic lessons work, versus what the souls can all do. Finding out what their purposes are. Let's say that there's a problem. Say the person comes in and says, 'I've been fighting with my sister for fifty years.' Sometimes it's really interesting to see how many lifetimes they've been fighting before that, or what caused the fight. Sometimes it's sort of like a little research project and getting to the root of something. Sometimes it's kind of a relief to get to the root of it. You can really feel like, oh, this is *this* way.

"I'll give you an example: I just had a woman who was a nurse, and I was doing a reading with her on the phone. She was having these strange blotches break out, and I could not *feel* any reason why these things were breaking out on her body, and I don't think the doctors could … What I kept seeing was a person who had died of, I think it was smallpox, in a previous life. She was in a particularly traumatic period in her life right [then], and she felt sort of screwed over by the world and abandoned and abused.

"What was interesting [in Mary's reading] was she had the smallpox, and the people came into the camp and realized that most every one of these Indians were dead except for her and, like, two others and, instead of helping them and re-hydrating them and giving them medicine, they just left. So this cruel abandonment that she went through, I felt like she was going through like emotions that were similar now … and so it was like, Ohhh, and *for me,* it's even like, oh, that's why they're [the blotches] coming out. So, for me, it's like, oh, that's interesting…

"She's in a particular place where she feels all of the similar emotions from that time, so I think as soon as she clicked into that vibration of pain, it started breaking out. But also her job—she's an RN who wants to be a holistic practitioner with her own practice and … her own body is the example. I think she's going through this thing so that she could know what to tell other people … so that she can be a very good practitioner out there and help a lot of people heal."

Mary once liked to read novels. Now she "reads" stories in a different way that is just as stimulating.

"For me, sometimes it's just like an education. I learn so much from people that is interesting. I used to love to read; I haven't been able to read as much … but what's interesting is, this is sort of like reading, [but] instead of reading books or novels, this is like reading life stories. I mean, you learn a lot from these life stories. They're always interesting. There's not too many boring ones."

All clients, however, do not want their soul story told, Mary said.

"There are people who don't want you to read the life story. 'Don't talk about reincarnation. Don't talk about why my soul's here. I just want to know how my business is going to do.' Those readings are fine, but they're not nearly as interesting as these other ones. Because, once again, it's almost like, the stuff that people go through, you couldn't make up.

"Like these people walking into this camp of Indians ... back a hundred and something years ago and seeing most of them dead and then a couple alive, and abandoning them. I mean, it's a very disappointing segment of history, very sad, but it's interesting because it does come back around. This person still is working out the pain of some of that stuff.

"It really is an education about how every single thing we do, however small it is, however big it is, really makes a huge impact. If somebody had just helped these people, this woman probably would not be going through the trauma she's going through. So, look at all the people *now* going through trauma that we're not doing anything about ... It's *hugely* interesting."

Weeding Out Clients

Mary has found that people who are only interested in mundane matters are somewhat boring readings for her, and often the readings are ineffective. Eventually, she set up a message on her telephone answering system to alert potential clients to the fact that she focuses on life lessons and life purpose.

"That's how I sort of weed people out," Mary said.

If people are not interested in what they're here to do and to learn, Mary said, there are plenty of good psychics out there who focus on other things, and those clients are better off to find one of those psychics.

"The ones that *I* would like to get readings from are the ones who would be interested in looking at the internal workings of the soul, as I am, or the soul history, and the way the human race is."

As with most intuitives who attune to higher levels for information, Mary does not believe she is supposed to read for everyone who seeks to come before her. Sometimes it is not the right time to read for a certain person; whereas, another time might be ideal.

"I know I don't feel every reading is meant to be. I feel like the people who are meant to be there are there, and the people who are not, aren't ... It's got to be a certain energy attraction ... When the right time happens, it'll be there."

How She Works

Mary explains how the information comes to her when she gives a reading.

"See," she said. "Hear now. Basically, I'll see a little bit. I might see an image to start off the picture; I might sense something. I don't see pictures of people ... I sense the essence of the soul much more than the essence of personality ... much more easily than, say, the physical description ... I can get a sense of how they interact, a sense of what they value, a sense of who they are, a sense of what the kinds of things they've done with their time and their lives [are], that kind of thing. So that's, I guess, what's interesting to me ... I don't recognize people the way they *look* ... it's what I *feel* about them."

Rather than hearing things clairaudiently, or seeing pictures clairvoyantly, it is as if Mary gets into a flow of information.

"Sometimes I do hear it and I do sort of *know* it ... I'd say 90 percent of it is more an intuition, which is coming from a higher source, and some of it is psychic-ness, which is coming from the soul of the other person. Psychic is of the soul, so psychic is of the soul of the other person. Intuition is from God.

"So that combination—because the soul will tell you what it needs you to know. The personality—the person'll sit there and tell you what *they* want you to tell!" Mary said, laughing lightly. "But the soul is psychic, so your psychic-ness is of the soul. You're tuning into the soul of the person, not their personality, not necessarily what their personality wants to hear, even," she said and again laughed.

"And then, intuition is really from God, so that's the higher consciousness that's holding us all together, that [we] actually all interact with all the time and we don't know it. But that God consciousness is always directing, is always a part of the reading, whether it's very verbal on one day or less verbal on another. That can change, but it is directing it. So, there are different sources of information. So yes, the soul being the main source …"

Mary doesn't necessarily feel that she works with specific guides or intermediaries from the other side.

"I'm plugging into the higher consciousness of the person, and I'm plugging into God," she reiterated. "I'd rather go straight to the highest sources. There probably are guardians or guides or angels helping … because I always ask them to come in.

"Some psychics are very tuned into guides, are very tuned into guardians like angels … I believe in the angels; I know that they're there. And I do tend to sense some of the angels sometimes, and sometimes I'll tune into people and oh the room suddenly fills up; I can *feel* a lot of other people or beings around. I can feel something. I don't see them though. Again, not being clairvoyant can be a little bit of a disadvantage because I don't really *see* like other people see … Probably, by the end of this lifetime, if I live long enough, I would have developed more of it, because I do have more of it now than I did, say, fifteen years ago."

If anything, Mary is claircognizant, which is the gift of clear knowing.

"I know things," she affirmed. "And knowing is intuition. I just get a sense of a whole concept … a whole sense of an energy. But I do feel that there's a God consciousness working with every reading, and the soul is working with every reading, and one thing I will say about the readings is, I think that they can be positive in that the potential of the soul to express itself through that particular body is extraordinary.

"If people are in touch with their potential—not what they *think* they want, not what their neediness is saying for them to do, but their real, higher potential, their real deeper fulfillment, those are very positive readings."

Through the soul, Mary has seen the possibility of a greater tomorrow that is attainable.

"We're all working out problems. We're all working out stress. We're all working out issues and lessons, but what's interesting is that the potential of the soul is so extraordinary that we could have much more extraordinary lives than we're having … Once we get past ourselves, past our lessons, past our individual, you know, garbage, that we bring in that we all have to work on ... Once you get past that—it feels like the next thing—people can really, really be happy here ... and live on a higher level of development."

The Mechanics of Giving a Reading

Mary's husband is a writer, and, in watching him work, Mary has come to believe that his craft is akin to her own.

"That kind of continuity that you have with writing is the same kind of concentration that you use for a reading, and as soon as you lose your continuity or the concentration in a reading, you could lose the whole conceptual thought right there. So actually, the writing and the reading are probably somehow related psychically. They're probably energetic cousins of some kind," she suggested.

"Some people say readings don't tire them out. Well, I think if you do them all the time and you do them full-time, they *do* tire you out because it's extreme concentration. The only other people I've met that I think actually concentrate to this level ... work in translating ... When we were doing conferences and programs in Japan, what was interesting was, they had to change translators every ... two hours ... I talked with a translator, and she said, 'Oh my gosh, my brain is broken.'

"They were so busy, so deeply concentrating on everything with the English language and trying to get the thoughts and the ideas right ... it took such astute concentration to do that, to keep the continuity of thought in both languages ...

"It's the same kind of concentration."

Because giving readings can be so taxing, in order to maintain a healthy, balanced state, Mary now works to strengthen her body.

"It actually helped me to start physically working out more and lifting weights ... and I think it's because the body hasn't been fatigued; it's been sitting down in a chair for six hours. I think that's one of the problems for those of us who do this. There's almost a mandatory exercise, which I'm sure everyone knows that they should do, and of course a lot of people like me, we did it when we felt like doing it. And it turns out that things have gone much better since I have consistently exercised, because it really wears and fatigues and balances the body with the spirit energy ... and then the sleep is better, and everything else goes better because of it. I do think that ... you need to fatigue the body to the same degree that the brain is fatigued."

Prayer, Protection, and Meditation

Mary discussed the role prayer plays in her work.

"I will say the Our Father. I make them up myself ... I have specific things I ask for each reading. I do say some of the same things, and then, sometimes, I ask things for certain readings. It's like, 'Okay, well, we need to know about this,' or 'We need to be able to get in touch with this person that's passed away' ... Say in a reading somebody says, 'I want to know about how my sister's doing because she died,' then I will add that in as part of my prayer: 'This person really needs to know, so I ask the sister to come in and help us out so we can create healing here.' So I do specific [prayers] based on what I know of that they're [clients] going to need.

"And then, I have a general prayer that I do that's a relatively lengthy prayer for all readings, for getting information about the soul, for getting information about what's going to help them the most, what's going to be healing and fulfilling for them. Then I always do the Lord's Prayer or I always say the Our Father ... That's the one I will always say because it seems like it's the one that opens the chakras most. Sometimes I will say it more than once.

"And certain prayers, if I do sense an angel around or somebody else who's a helper or guardian, I'll ask them specifically, 'Can you make sure that when you're working with me you help me interpret what you're saying to me, to help me interpret your information properly?' Because I do have to interpret it, and I can screw that up, so that's why it's good—why I always ask for God to help me interpret properly. I always ask for the angels to help me interpret properly, because ... you can get the information, but if you don't interpret it properly ... it's not useful."

Mary prays silently.

"I never say them out loud. Because not everybody wants to hear it, number one. Number two, I don't think they need to hear it. But, also, I think it's part of my internal process for tuning in. It's just something,

I don't know how it came around, it just came around over, maybe, the first year I was doing it … Somewhere in the first year I always said the prayer, a certain prayer, an organized religion prayer, but this … I almost started doing it automatically. I'm not sure why or where it even came from … because I've done it for so long."

If and when Mary feels a need for additional protection, she takes certain actions.

"I've done some smudging. I've used some frankincense; frankincense is a pretty good incense for cleaning. If I have a real problem in here, a problem person or a problem reading, I'll clean everything out. Most of the people aren't problems, most of the people I work with, they may *have* problems, but they're not problem people; they don't bring that lower darker energy in. The very few that have, I can clean it out. But I do prayers, and if I do speak to a person who is in spirit who is not a relative or a friend, I'll tell them at the end, 'Okay, you can go with your loved one, go with your daughter, go with your son, go with your sister' … I kind of send them on their way and they don't usually want to stay."

Mary does not meditate so much since her son came along.

"Not much anymore. Not since I had the baby. I try to do it sometimes. I haven't had a lot of quiet time for three years. I used to do more meditation. I used to love doing meditation and resting at the beach. I could really tune into myself, I could really get centered … and really feel cleansed and whole and well. I always found the beach to be a very, very positive place to go … I also find that the working out is its own meditation, because when you're in your own space doing these things, there's nothing but you and God and space anyway. I do try to do some walking, and the walking is sort of like a walking meditation. I just sort of go out and be with nature …"

Soul Purpose and Life Lessons

Mary was asked to describe how she gets out of the way in order to connect with the soul of the person she is reading for.

"Basically, once I get in here and we get settled down, I'll tune into them through the photograph or through holding the jewelry … You really do have to get yourself out of the way, and there's certain prayers that I say ... and a lot of the prayers that I do are to protect both of us.

"I have a certain intention that I have for all the readings, and so I say that intention in the prayers, and ... that the soul talks to me and that we communicate accurately and get as much information that's helpful to the person, that's actually healing to the person.

"I have certain things that I say in my head, and there's a certain place—some people call it alpha and some people will call it another state of mind—but once I get to that place, you can sort of feel a difference, very subtle, and then information starts coming through.

"Then, once I add my voice to the information, it starts to really multiply, it starts to move fast, and sometimes I don't know where I'm going with something."

Once Mary begins talking, she doesn't quite know where she's going, but she generally ends up at a place where she can speak of that soul's purpose.

She postulated that the last age, the Piscean Age, was very lesson-oriented and that, generally, we each had an agenda we came to execute. She feels that many of us have learned those lessons and that we're now at a point where we can be more in charge of creating our lives and tending more to our souls' purposes.

"I feel like people's lives are moving into a place where they're becoming more co-creative with God. They're more helping create their lives. They're more able to get out of their own way ...

"I think once you move through a lesson, you're done. You may have several tests on the lesson to get rid of it, but then you're going to be done with it, and once you master a lesson, you're finished. That becomes wisdom, and you can move on into other things."

With a person's life lessons increasingly out of the way, the soul's purpose can be more fully expressed and explored.

"I just feel like that's what souls are beginning to do, to express themselves more through the body. What I'm interested in, mostly, is the soul ... So the stuff I like to look at is what the soul is here for ...

"Life purpose and soul mission, that's very interesting stuff *to me,* and every soul has one, so I've always been able to tap into that, and if people ask for it, I can get it. Sometimes I get it if they don't ask for it. But that's the stuff that I think is really, really fascinating for a soul to be involved with, because when you get into that stuff, fulfillment is inevitable."

By fulfillment Mary is not referring to some of the current media hype, which suggests that such may be found in outer things and appearances.

"It's about being who you really need to be as the soul ... Everybody has a role. When you go back to the question [about] what's good about doing this work, [it] is finding out that every single person I've ever worked with has something to do here that's significant and unique to themselves."

Much of Mary's work has to do with helping people through great difficulties. She does not want to minimize people's pain, but underlying the pain is the marvelous tapestry of each person's unique being.

"Is it fun to work with parents whose children have died? No, that's not fun ... Is it fun to work with people who are so grieved that they can barely get a breath because they're crying so much? No, that's not fun. There's no counselor out there, and I'm sure there's no psychic out there who takes it seriously who will tell you that that's easy work. There are situations that I've worked with that I've had nightmares about ... There are some ... elements of the human race that are so difficult to work with and are so painful for humans that it does bother me.

"I'm saying there is that difficult stuff that people go through ... but then there's that beauty and originality of each soul that also is extraordinary, even souls that are going through tremendous difficulty still have that on their side, that they can eventually focus on again. Maybe not in the first reading, if we do that, maybe I won't be the one that focuses on it with them, maybe I'm there to do something else. But that originality of the soul, that expression of the soul, is a most interesting thing."

An Easy Acceptance of Reincarnation

On some level Mary has always known about reincarnation. Even before she was exposed to it, she knew there were certain things she didn't want to have to do again.

"I always believed in it actually; it always made sense to me. I think the first book I read ... was in college ... I think it was Gina Cerminara's

Many Mansions: The Edgar Cayce Story on Reincarnation, and it *totally* made sense to me ...

"I remember being a little kid, having to get shots. I hated shots, and I used to have a big fit about [it]. I remember thinking, 'I can't do this again!' I don't want to have to do it again [in a future life] ... "

Mary had early exposure to the notion of reincarnation, through her studies.

"So much of astrology sort of allowed for the idea of a past life. It's mentioned in so many astrology [references]. It wasn't a huge emphasis, but it was there."

Also, when she was a drama teacher, Mary said one of the mothers brought her three-year-old to class, and the child appeared to have some past life recall. Mary thinks this reminded her of what she already knew.

"I was exposed very young, when I was teaching drama, to a mother whose son was having reincarnation [flashbacks]. I was twenty-three, and I was teaching drama at this summer program, and the woman was alarmed because a three-year-old boy came up with a story. Her husband was a staunch conservative and she said, 'My son just came up and said this and I heard you do readings.' I was doing them more as a hobby at the time and very, very part-time, but she knew I had ...

"She said her son was telling a story to them about being in a log cabin and that he had died in this log cabin. It was snowing, and his brothers had gone out, and they were all forestry people ... I guess lumbermen, lumberjacks, or something. The two brothers went out, and they must have got caught in a huge storm, and they both died, and the third brother was supposed to go out, and he ended up starving to death in the cabin. Anyway, the kid knew things that he shouldn't have known—like there are certain things you use for maple syrup, certain barrels. The way this kid described these barrels, this woman went and researched it and found out that these barrels were used by people who were lumber people ... This mother was very upset. I'm thinking, well I think it must be true then, why would the kid make it up, and how could he possibly know how the barrels were used ...

"And even by that time I was totally comfortable with it, and that was just after college."

In Mary's work, reincarnation is a keystone, and seeing past lives comes easily to her.

Past Lives, or Reading the Whole Soul History

Doing past life readings is among the easiest things for Mary.

"I must have a real soul affinity with that stuff, because that stuff is the easiest I get," she said. "Sometimes, in order to see the future, I look at a past. Sometimes, when I want to see where they're going, I look at the past to see where they've been. The whole soul history is one line. I know people think it's a broken-up line, because they're alive now and they've been dead and they've been in another life, but it's one line. Some lifetimes, very clearly, are connected to the life you're in … And the ones that are truly, deeply connected to their life purpose this time are the ones that are very interesting to me …

"The soul history, in and of itself, both in lifetimes in the body and outside of the body, is fascinating, because the soul is busy; it's always doing something. Even when you die, you're doing something. And that can be why death can be hard to read, because people may be dead, but they're still busy. People actually have plenty of stuff to do after they're out of their body. Some people don't, because they didn't do a lot when they were alive," she said and giggled. "So some people are busier than others, just like it is when they're alive."

Mary learned to attune herself to the eternal records that are written on the scrolls of the ethers of space.

"The past life stuff is fascinating. It's all the Akashic Records. And I know some … psychics have been known to say, 'I read the Akashic Records,' but the Akashic Records are all there *is* to read. There isn't anything else."

Akashic is a Sanskrit word, and the Akashic Records are said to be the eternal records that are written on etheric scrolls.

"It's like, that's all there is," Mary said. "That is the essence of the soul history, that's the fabric of time and space and everything outside of time and space. That's it, that's it, there is nothing else *to* read. It is the soul history.

"But past lives are just easy to read … I just see them. I see those really clearly … I must have been here a few times … That's why I think I can read them so easily. I must have been around, in and out of these lifetimes a lot myself. I don't think I was a witness; I think I was a participant."

Even though Mary supposes that she is reading the so-called Akashic Records, she doesn't necessarily refer to them as that.

"I'm inclined to call it the soul history, the essence of the soul as it goes through time. But like I said, not all lives are pertinent to this life. You could do a reading for a person and never pick up on certain lifetimes. Then, you could do five readings for a person, say, over fifteen years and pick up on different lifetimes because they're at different phases of their life, doing different things that call on one of those lifetimes. As the busier souls have been and out of these lifetimes, they've got more lifetimes to call on.

"It isn't all tragic. Some of it is downright interesting, and some of it's pretty fun."

Mary enjoys doing past life regressions.

"I've done past life regression a couple of times myself. I rather like past life regression because the detail comes through in a very personal way; whereas, when I'm reading, I'm reading it from the outside and skipping over some stuff and going faster through some things and getting into detail in other areas. When you're in a past life regression, you're *in* that life, and you're seeing every bit of detail, from the pottery to the shoes on your feet. When I'm doing a reading, I don't care about the shoes on their feet. I already know what era we're in. I already know where we're going with the ideas and with the overall thoughts and intentions."

Generally, someone trained to do them facilitates past life regressions.

"They're usually people who've been trained in hypnosis, hypnotherapy, and they usually have certifications … I think there's more therapists getting that …

"Ten years ago or eight years ago, I was going to a therapist, and we were looking at some past lives to see what had happened to me with certain situations, why I reacted the way I did. It was really interesting because the past life gave tremendous detail. I really do enjoy some of the hypnotherapy, because we're in that lighter state of hypnosis where you're just going through it and looking ... or you're seeing a detail that you could never make up."

Mary said people can conduct these regressions by themselves, but they might want to have someone on hand to assist.

"Everybody can do their own readings and be accurate," Mary said. "That's a good place to learn about yourself ... You just have to find a qualified practitioner to help you, to coach you through that process, because that's a process you definitely need somebody else to do with you. There are some tapes that allow people to do readings/regressions by themselves, but you also have to turn off the phone, and you should do prayers ahead of time so that you don't bring in any energies you don't want to bring in. I mean, you want to make sure it stays clean. So you can do it on your own, but I always liked having the practitioner around too."

What She Doesn't Tell, Why Good Psychics Err, and Getting Self-Guidance

Mary doesn't get any information that she feels she should not disclose to the client.

"I don't get anything ...A lot of time people come to me, and they're already in crisis or in the middle of a divorce or their marriage is already failing ... So is it something that you don't talk about? No, you talk about it. In the last ten or fifteen years, I think I've gotten better at being more honest about what the outcome could be ... If you do this, this could happen. If you don't get counseling—I would say I'm a big advocate for counseling. I have found that if anybody is willing to work on anything, they probably can heal it to a degree that would surprise them, and it would be a pleasant surprise.

"So I would say, I don't hold anything back ... I focus more on the positive, on coming out with the positive healing."

Mary conceded that often even good intuitives are simply wrong.

"I'll tell you where I've been wrong is timing. Timing's tricky," she said. "As far as general predictions and being wrong, I'd say sometimes ... we're just wrong. Sometimes I do feel that people don't do what they can do to change something. They're holding on to something, or they're using their free will. Say they're holding on to a marriage, and they know that it's not going that well, and, either they're not willing to get therapy for themselves or to get help for … the marriage.

"I think a lot of time there are situations where I'll say, 'Well this could come out this way, but you need to do x, y, and z.' And they don't do the x, y, and z. Or they do the best that they can, and there may be other people involved with the decision.

"So I do think free will and other people's free will probably plays somewhat into it, but as far as being wrong, I've never been able to figure out being really off. Because I know Edgar Cayce had been really off, predicted several things that didn't actually happen at the time that he said. And I do think it could have been the world consciousness change, because he was doing national, world affairs readings, and stuff … Even now, I still think there are so many different people playing in to [affect] something on the level of, like, world affairs, that maybe it did change the outcome."

Mary talked about how she gets guidance for herself and about how much she wants to know.

"Sometimes I'll do a reading, actually do a reading … I think as you get older and you get more and more into this stuff, you start to *know* things. And I also have made conscious decisions about what I want to know and what I don't want to know. There are certain things I don't want to know.

"When I was younger I wanted to know everything, and I think that was probably stupid to a degree. It's not good to know everything, I don't think. Knowing about death or certain things, I don't think we're really well prepared to handle …

"*Now* I would like to know, maybe generally, certain things, and I'd be open to getting readings sometimes from other people. I've met some psychics; I've liked their vibration. I've liked who they seemed to be. I certainly ask my partner Linda [Schiller-Hanna] for readings, sometimes, when I've been having a problem."

Mary is now conducting classes with others through ARE, but she taught with Linda for a long time.

"As a matter of fact … we've had a problem with mold in the house in the last year, and I was sick all the time. She [Linda] kept calling me saying, 'My god, you're sick again … ' My son was always sick, and we couldn't figure it out. One day she called and I was coughing and hacking again. We had another [teaching] program to do … and she's like, 'You can't keep being this sick' … and she said, 'Look, let's do a reading on this.' The first thing she says is, 'I get mold. It's not you. It's not your immune system. It's mold in your house. You really gotta do something about it.'

"And she was dead-on right.

"I will say, I was suspicious. It was something I was sort of considering and starting to come around to [the idea of], but I'd never mentioned it to her. I never said, 'This is my suspicion …' I just let her do this thing.

"So I think that part of it is being open to other people helping you … As long as it doesn't become an addiction. When I was younger, I think it was something I did too often, and so I stopped getting all readings for a very long period. I didn't get any readings from anybody for a good ten years, maybe longer."

Mary simply had enough and wanted to live the life, not know about it.

"I didn't *want* any readings from anybody; I wanted to just work stuff out for myself. And then, just recently, I got more open, and once again my friend [Linda] … we do little reading exchanges and stuff. I know her very well and she knows me relatively well, so there's a lot of trust there. But she's been dead-on accurate about some of the stuff that's been going on with me. So if I do get to a place where I need help, I'll ask for it …

"I'm trying to be more open to other people, because I have run into a number of psychics that I don't think we would necessarily click.

"As far as tuning in, I try to live it now and be more conscious about being tuned in to what's going on … There's a crisis in my family right now, and we're trying to work with it. Once again, I don't want a reading on the outcome. I don't want any of that stuff, but I'm trying to be conscious about how I'm working with it, so I can live with it and just keep working with it the way it is."

Mary considered how often she thinks someone should have a reading.

"It depends on if they're going through a crisis or what. You could have one reading, and that could be it. You don't necessarily need more. Because if you're doing the basic life purpose [reading], then go off and do it! So it may be that they ... may not need the support psychically because they don't have as many obstacles to fulfilling their life purpose. They may be really in a flow place. Sometimes people are in that place, and they just call back a year later and say, 'Yeah, I'm just checking in.' They're all different."

The Best, Highest Use of One's Psychic Ability

Like most high-level intuitives, Mary said there have been people she couldn't read for, or wasn't supposed to. She has strong opinions on what she thinks a psychic of her caliber is supposed to be doing, which is to help people improve themselves and their situations and, therefore, the world.

"I have had a couple of people I felt like I couldn't read in my life. I remember saying to one guy—this is about fourteen years ago—'Well I think that we should probably not do this, this isn't working out,' and he said, 'Well, I really need to know something' ... It was all about business and money and stuff like that and that was his agenda ... So it was perfectly legitimate for me to talk to him about it ... but I also felt like he was not really interested in spirituality or anything else deeper.

"He was really interested in himself, so what I found was that the reading stopped. And it stopped hard. There was no place to go. He wasn't particularly interested in his life purpose; he wasn't particularly interested in doing anything else with the human race; he wasn't particularly interested in anything else, so I felt like I was really dead-ended from the beginning.

"There's a few people—I've had probably three incidents in the twenty years I've worked—where I've felt that dead end, and that was the first time I felt it from the beginning."

Mary decided it was better for all concerned if she informed prospective clients at the outset about her primary focus in giving readings.

"That's why I'm very clear about what I do [soul purpose and life lessons], and I don't really want to attract anybody [looking for something else]..."

She said the client mentioned above had a different agenda, so it did not work for her to read for him.

"I feel like the stuff I'm really good at or the stuff I'm really interested in is the human race doing something for somebody else, being of service for somebody else, actually becoming better beings, because that's my sort of place that I'm trying to come from ... For example, this person didn't want to better any of his relationships, he didn't really care how anybody else felt, he was just like, 'You guys take it or leave it, I don't care what you think.' And because his attitude was so self-centered and so incredibly selfish ... there was no point in talking about it. So I was very dead-ended."

Mary said if she works with people who fall within a certain vibrational range, it's better for all concerned.

"I never saw him again, which was actually really good ... I do think ... we all vibrate at a certain level and we're supposed to work within a certain vibrational *range*. I find that the range that I like to work with, they are interested in life purpose. They are interested in bettering themselves and the world. They are interested in broadening themselves. They are interested in doing something for somebody besides themselves, even though they could be interested in themselves too. They could have both interests, but [not be] deeply selfish and deeply cruel or deeply vindictive."

That gentleman wasn't the only difficult case Mary has had, but it helped to teach her what works best for her.

"But I just think that there are certain vibrations that we're not supposed to get [into]. It's a kind of intimate connection, and I do think for the psychic's protection, we need to stay ... within the ranges that we can work with. For our own sanity. I think the more you work with the public at large, you start to broaden the range, and you might go lower than you should go, vibrationally."

Mary would like to see psychics use their abilities to try to better situations and people, not just to help people get rich or the like. A higher calling warrants a higher output.

"I really do feel psychic work is more about connecting souls together and doing things for the world and working toward oneness and love. I don't feel that psychic work is really about helping people whose agendas are purely selfish. I don't think we're supposed to be using our psychic talent that way. I'm not sure that's what it's supposed to be about, that's why I think some psychics do burn out because they may run into too many of those people. They may get too well known in some cases and end up working with too many people who have genuinely selfish agendas.

"There's lots of creative people and wonderful people out there, and people who really are just working their life out as best they can. They're easy to read, they're good to read. You can work with those guys. There's lots of them out there. But there's other ones that would use a psychic for their … own selfish [ends]."

As for Mary, she finds it's best to steer clear of selfish clients, lest the depth and breadth of what she can reach is diluted.

A New Heaven, a New Earth

Mary still sometimes has a problem with feeling other people's stuff when she doesn't want to, and she has a sense of why this is.

"That's still hard, because there are some people that I've been around, I'll realize it's them and it's not me, and I still run into that sometimes. I think it's because the tension here is so high, it's so difficult nowadays. It is so stressful, so many people are having crises, so many people are having issues … There's a lot of that going on … with people where they just feel like nobody cares about their problems and that kind of thing. I just feel like there's a lot of loneliness and isolation with people. So I actually feel like they're acting it out in all kinds of ways, and I feel like they're pushing it out of their energy field more powerfully than they ever used to."

Because of the way Mary works, which is to help people with their spiritual growth, some clients simply want to check in and make sure everything is on track with them. Others, however, are seeking to abate a sense of loneliness and disconnection that is nearly chronic at this time. Mary believes our sense of loneliness and isolation may be purposeful in that it can cause us to reach for God and to do more for others than we've ever done before.

"I run into a lot of women who are married who feel desperately alone, but they're married … And people I run into … where they're deeply lonely in their lives, but they're around people all the time. But there's no connection, or the connections are poor, or the connections are failing.

"So I do think a lot of people see psychics ... because we're the only connections they have. Psychologists probably are in that boat too, where people are calling them and seeing them because the people ... feel the loneliness in a profound way.

"So like I said, I've just seen a lot of people who are lonely but they're around people, but they're not connected emotionally or spiritually to the people that are around. So you've got to wonder. That relationship [marriage] can be healed, but they have to want to heal it. Find something in common or do something where they both have something in common.

"There's a deep loneliness out there. It really is profound."

Mary sees a number of reasons for it.

"I think technology's part of it. I also think part of it is we're going through a period where ... it's a testing of the soul. I actually feel a lot of people are going through sort of a dark night of the soul period ... to get rid of a lot of their old karmic patterns and to move up into a higher vibration. I think people feel very tested right now. It's like they've been going through that testing of the dark night."

The dark night of the soul is said to be a time of spiritual testing when it seems as if others have turned away from us, and even God seems difficult to reach.

"I noticed loneliness there twenty years ago. I think, also, because people are so busy, they don't have enough time for themselves, they don't have enough space to themselves, they don't play anymore. *Kids* don't play anymore."

Mary said splintered communities, with families split up and living in various places, is another contributor to a near-chronic sense of loneliness and isolation among the masses. In some regard, she thinks it is an opportunity for humanity.

"We've lost our neighborhoods and we've lost our communities ... And there are a lot of people that are feeling alone, and there's an awful lot of people that end up alone, because most of their family died off or moved away, or they've gone in different directions, don't have the same interests. So, it's like we have to rebuild our community, our individual communities.

"I think the twenty-first century's an opportunity to rebuild our community, whether it's a family community, or I think we have to decide who's within our family, because our family could be our friends, it could be people that we're connected to, it can be people that we care about. We just have to rebuild it. I think it used to be based on genetic ties: who your family members were, and who the neighbors and your friends were. Now I think a lot of that's changed … now I think it's about rebuilding a community based on similar interests, similar needs, similar vibrations. I think it's hard work, but it does feel like people are working on a lot of karmic lessons, a lot of difficulties."

Mary also believes the sense of loneliness people feel is purposeful in that it provides us with an impetus to reach for a stronger personal relationship with God.

"I think that it's part of the things and lessons that people are going through right now, where they really are on their own between the human race and God … It's an opportunity to turn more to God."

We have an opportunity to become more of a co-creator with God, Mary thinks, and perhaps to build a heaven on earth.

"It feels like it's about learning to live on a higher vibration, you know like heaven and spirit, like heaven's a spiritual idea, when you die and go to heaven. I think our job is to make—and Cayce said this— to make earth more like a heaven. Earth is *meant* to be more of a heavenly place. I do feel that part of our job is to create this place to be more heavenly, to be more perfect, to be more cooperative, to be more of a positive place.

"I think with the experience that we have, each soul, we have a fulfillment that makes it. I think right now we're unconscious of our fulfillment somehow. We're part of God but God isn't fully functioning through us. Part of my understanding is that God created us so that we could be co-creators with Him, but we're not co-creators until we really know what we're doing, until we really have experiences where we actually have to learn about the law of cause and effect. We actually have to learn how the universe works. We have to learn how to control our tempers. We have to learn how to be better people. We have to learn to be more giving. We have to learn to be more loving. So I do feel that the higher the vibrations become, the more loving we become, the more perfect we become as human beings, the closer to God we are. So maybe ultimately, it's to become more like God.

"I think with all these different soul groups, all their talents and their expressions, all of us together will create a whole in the universe. All of us are not going to be the same. There is still individuality. It's almost like on earth we're expressing more individuality than we would've if we were in spirit and never came down here. And then, going back to God with that individuality that we've developed and perfected, then God becomes broader ... we become broader than we were, we're part of God, but we're *consciously* part of God. It's probably more complicated than that," she said and laughed. "In a nutshell that might be part of it."

"There's a lot of people calling though that still need the readings, who are still working through the transition that they need to go through to get to the Aquarian Age. They talk about this, they talk about vibration raising. There was a lot of vocabulary applied to this that I didn't love because it made it sound very flaky. I'm not a fan of flaky language. I'm not a fan of some of the stuff I heard in the seventies and the eighties about some of this stuff, but I'd say that this is really a shift in consciousness and that's what I would call it, a shift in consciousness. I would bill it as consciousness raising ...

"I know that this experience of moving into this time is about people becoming more responsible, more co-creative, more aware of their neighbor, more people more with love and less with power. I think it's actually really nice, I think it's going to be great—we just have to get there! And then, we have to be responsible once we're there. We can't just forget everything we learned; we can't just go backwards, because if you go backwards, you'll just end up back at the beginning of all your work.

"It really does have to be said, I think, it will ultimately be a positive outcome. The Aquarian Age is going to be a positive age where people will be able to do more with their lives, be more conscious, be more co-creative, be more responsible, and I think will be able to do more for other people than we have ever. Ever. Ever in the history of the human race."

AFTERWORD

In doing the research for this book I had many adventures with the psychics and intuitives whose services I sought. They told me things that made me burst out laughing and shared knowings that stunned me.

When I realized I wanted to pursue this project, I enlisted family and friends to get readings from the people I was considering interviewing. I solicited their opinions about their sessions and listened to recordings of the sessions or read the transcripts. I myself had multiple readings with each of the psychics and intuitives in the book.

I found consulting with these unconventional professionals to be a great help yet at times perhaps something of a hindrance. Their offerings were often illuminating and encouraging, and many, many times they moved me to tears with the insights they provided. At times they steered me in directions that were perhaps not the best for me—if such a thing can be determined by looking back. Sometimes I took their advice; sometimes I didn't. They saved me from calamities and stunned me into speechlessness by echoing some of my deepest sentiments.

They told me about gifts I have that I am meant to share. They voiced my own sense of things many times, thereby empowering me to believe in myself more.

It was mostly fun to experience and experiment. Before each appointment I would wonder, *What will this one say? What insights might she offer? How does he work? What will she say about what has gone before? What surprises will I have? How keen are their skills?*

Some of the psychics and intuitives were especially useful in providing advice regarding general life affairs. They advised me on matters perhaps minor in the greater scheme of things, but still of interest and value.

It was fun and a little daunting to visit with all of these psychics and intuitives in so short a time. I am strongly on guard against those who are inclined to be negative; I'm afraid of what they might slip into my mind. Anyone having a psychic reading should proceed with caution.

I learned a number of things about these professionals along the way. All of them are different. They appear to work on different levels and to receive guidance from different sources (that are sometimes ultimately the same). At the very least, they work in different ways. Some are valuable only for a single session; after they gave what they got, they seemed unable to mine more of me in subsequent sessions.

As I zeroed in on the professionals to be profiled in this book, I focused on the ones who seemed to work on the higher levels. I don't think anyone said anything that scared me. There were times when things were said that concerned me, but within the telling of the matter of concern was a resolution to it.

In determining the psychics and intuitives to be profiled here, most of the consultations were conducted over the phone, which is amazingly effective. As for conducting the actual interviews, I went on site to visit with each of the chosen seven, except for one who I already knew and another who I met later. In those instances we spoke only by phone. In some cases I spent days with the persons, and in every instance I spoke with the individual for hours.

As I sorted from among the best of the best, I found striking similarities. Mary Roach said when you get to a certain level, you all have access to the same information, and she may be right. It is only a few who are able to operate at that level, however. Most of the psychics who work on the higher levels stress positivity, which in and of itself is a blessing.

In the end, however, I decided that even good readings and good readers should be used sparingly unless you have a sense of being in a crisis, and then their guidance can be invaluable, if for no other reason than to help you put things in perspective and regain your equilibrium. In getting readings for this work, there were times when my head would spin. In considering my own life affairs, I would think, *Well, so-and-so said this—but such-and-such said that.* I didn't like it. I felt disempowered and missed my own good judgments. Even the opinions of my family and friends seemed less worthy in light of my intuitive contacts. After an onslaught of sessions for a prolonged period, in some ways it was as if I had to re-train myself to trust my own judgment and hone my own intuitive skills.

At times I realized that many good things offered to me in past sessions hadn't been used up—that there was still noble, elevated guidance that I hadn't quite gotten to. In getting so many readings, it became as if I was looking for the next pleasing pronouncement that excited me or bobbed me to the surface of self-doubt. Therefore, I question the value of frequent psychic sessions.

However, there were so many highlights—more than not, certainly. I was advised when close relatives were troubled, which helped prompt me to reach out to them. As well, I was assured when others whom I held concerns for were doing well.

Some of the psychics and intuitives dared to tell me the main reasons I came into this lifetime, causing my heart to soar with joy at the prospect of achieving those goals and to tremble with trepidation at the possibility that I might not.

I was helped to understand why there was a distance between myself and another, so that as I understood the ways in which we did not understand each other, I could accept what was and thereby bridge the gulf.

More than one advised me when it was best to keep my own counsel, lest sharing details of my plans or activities would attract others' contrary thoughts and possibly hamper the unfolding of something beneficial to me.

I was given useful advice regarding my physical well being.

It was not uncommon to get conflicting advice. If you are considering getting a psychic reading and can afford it, it may be best to get two or three. All psychics and intuitives—except perhaps the "sleeping" Edgar Cayce who so completely stepped out of the way—

have to filter the information that comes to them through the lens of their own opinions and experiences, which can color the information. But I've found that when I'm lost or confused, people who efficiently and ethically practice the divinatory arts can pull me from the morass of difficulty and help reset my inner compass.

I found it useful to consult with someone new at times. A new practitioner may have a fresh perspective and not hold you to previous patterns or expectations. Even one shining insight you can take away from a session can be more than enough.

Because I tended to work with people whose views are positive, seeking guidance from them was largely joyous. There were times when I followed their pronouncements eagerly, like a sorely needed a therapy session but with the benefit of insights and knowings, and they guided me well.

As for past life readings, many years ago I incorporated reincarnation into my belief system, yet few people can capably reach the storehouse where records of our past lives are kept. There is little doubt when someone accurately relates an account of a life you have lived, especially if it was a significant life. You resound with a sense of remembrance quite unlike anything previously experienced. Some of the psychics profiled in this book spoke to me of past lives that had such a resounding ring of truth that I was moved to tears, even when it was awkward and embarrassing.

They spoke of lofty goals set for myself and held in some secret vault of the all of me, heard like a distant remembrance of a promise once made to myself.

I conferred with some who described visions unfolding in their mind's eye and brought the account around to the summation of what it meant for me with such eloquence and aptness that I was deeply moved and inspired. They went beyond the everyday, to rarefied heights, and brought joy and profundity. They touched on my relationship with God and levels divine in ways no one had done—or known of. They spoke about things that reached so deeply that I was left to wonder, not just about what they said, but about their having access to such knowing.

As well, there are people not profiled in these pages who were highly impressive and gifted, especially in dealing with general life matters and minor but meaningful difficulties. I would like to acknowledge some of them. Susan Henson often gave useful, accurate information. Paula Vaughan was helpful with dreams and a quick knowing. Barbara Rasor helped me mine an emotional issue related to my original kidney injury, and important to me still. Norma Gentile is a gifted energetic healer. Atira Hatton often nailed it.

Divinatory practices, although ancient, are a relatively young art in current times. Such practices now offer elements of a young science since science is just beginning to look at the paranormal as valid. I used to say that the only reason scientists didn't believe in the supernatural was because they hadn't yet developed the instruments to measure it. That time has now passed, and a new science of the paranormal is emerging. Even physics is on board with the String Theory which, loosely put, says that many dimensions occupy the same space.

Perhaps this increasing appreciation of the supernatural reflects something that is going on with all of humanity. In her book *Kundalini and the Chakras*, Genevieve Lewis Paulson posits that humanity is on the precipice of a new evolutionary development. She theorizes that we are in the process of developing a fourth brain which relates to the intuitional level, and which already exists in the etheric above our heads and toward the back. It will enable us to tap into the Universal Mind and have "limitless potential for receiving information."

In some ways, it does seem that we have maximized the mental as we know it, from parsing legalese in our justice system, to our straining to *know*, and that the mental may be better utilized if enhanced by the intuitive.

Humanity appears poised and ready for this next step in its evolutionary development. If being psychic is using the senses to know and intuition is from God, the next stage of mankind's journey may be as cognizant co-creators and companions.

Divinatory, after all, has as its root the word *divine*.

I applaud the men and women who have worked with integrity on things beyond the ordinary at a time when to do so was not always easy. In their work, they opened doors for all of us—not just for those of us who have an interest in matters metaphysical or spiritual, but for all who follow. For when inroads are made, they remain as energetic pathways, even for subsequent generations. But someone has to first blaze those trails, to break through the underbrush, climb over boulders, and brave varied hazards.

These psychics and intuitives worked on things mysterious at a time when such pursuits were often looked at askance, and I salute them and those who came before them with gratitude.

Contact information for persons willing to provide it:

Golden Harp
c/o Serafina Andrews
PO Box 1073
Mendocino, CA 95460
707-964-6740
harpofgold.com

Barbara Friedkin
themysticofcavecreek.com

Norma Gentile
healingchants.com

Atira Hatton
206-767-5611
angelscribe.com/atira

Susan Henson
214-679-3098
972-575-8351
windspiritjourneys.com
susan@windspiritjourneys.com

Judith MacKenzie Castell
PO Box 203, Truro
N.S. Canada   B2N 5C1
800-730-5275
psychicintuitivejudymc.com

Barbara Rasor
949-689-8591
Assistant Professor
Holos University. Classes offered
at Holos University
Graduate Seminary.
holosuniversity.org

Mary Roach
PO Box 1469
Virginia Beach, VA 23451
757-426-6124

Catherine Rosek
719-488-9571
universalspiritualview.com

Paula Vaughan
303-447-0250
1133 Utica Circle
Boulder, CO 80304
paulavaughan.com
paula@paulavaughan.com

INDEX

Breinigsville, PA USA
19 December 2009
229521BV00001B/153/P